GW01045141

THE PORTRAITS
ON THE
WALL

FIVE CHERISHED PETS
FIVE SPECIAL STORIES

Zoë Jasko

Printed edition:
Also available in multiple e-book formats.

Published by:
The Endless Bookcase Ltd,
Suite 14 STANTA Business Centre, 3 Soothouse Spring,
St Albans, Hertfordshire, AL3 6PF, UK.

More information can be found at:
www.theendlessbookcase.com.

ISBN: 978-1-914151-70-5

Illustrations: **Peter Waine**

Cover Design: **Stephen Hill**

Author photo by **Andrew Mason**

For Stuart, my wonderful Dad.

I love you forever.

By the same author

*What The Wind Saw: Short Stories
from the Heart of Hertfordshire*

Hope is Daffodil Bright

ABOUT THE AUTHOR

Zoë's third book, *The Portraits on the Wall,* is a collection of five novella length stories inspired by portraits of imaginary pets. It follows hot on the heels of her first novel *Hope is Daffodil Bright* (The Endless Bookcase, 2023) and her first book, an anthology with a twist, *What the Wind Saw: Short Stories from the Heart of Hertfordshire* (The Endless Bookcase, 2022).

A trained singer, she is co-founder and creative director of the Hertfordshire-based Felici Opera, and now, in addition to performing, she enjoys turning her story telling skills to writing and speaking engagements.

Zoë has a BA in French and History (University of Exeter) and an MA in Victorian Studies - 19th Century art, history, and literature (Birkbeck College, University of London). She has been an active member of a marvellous book club since 2008.

She lives in Hertfordshire with her husband and four children.

www.zoejasko.com

Photo credit: Andrew Mason

I

ENDORSEMENTS

The imagery Zoë Jasko conjures up with her poetic language, where each sentence rises and falls like the cadence of a song to the rhythm of the heart, is every bit as rich and vivid a painting as the pet portraits from which she draws her initial inspiration. Her narrator describes the feeling of 'sitting at the edge of a picture, up close against the frame', but her prose takes us over that edge, right to the core of each scene. Her stories of love, friendship, acceptance, loss and personal growth stir more feelings than I can name, leaving my jaw aching from smiling and my eyes stinging with tears.

Anna McNay #TheCriticWithTheDog

Zoë has imagination in abundance and a talent at being able to keep the reader guessing until the very end and it's often unexpected and this, her latest book of five cherished pets, does exactly that. Each story is different and, as a pet lover, had me hooked, playing with the mind and heartstrings alike. I enjoyed them all, but if I had to choose a favourite, it would be 'Guy', as he was quite a character.

Zoë's books are for anyone wishing to escape, if only for a moment, and immerse themselves in the wonders of fiction, fact and fantasy and have been a pleasure to read and re-read.

Shelagh Fairbank, author and illustrator

This book will resonate instantly with all pet lovers. Zoë's prose effortlessly captures the many meaningful levels of mutual understanding between two equals. These portraits, both in prose and pictures - are a poignant manifestation and a permanent reminder of those unquestioning partnerships. A new classic has been safely delivered.

Peter Waine, author and illustrator

Winnie - what a beautiful story! Ultimately an uplifting tale about the never-ending bond between dog and human, and how this endures even through the brutality of war. Seen through the eyes of Anna, a freshly de-mobbed former WAAF member, the reader is taken through the emotional ups and downs of her recent life story told to an equally freshly demobbed soldier sharing the same railway carriage. There is fear, despair, anger, and tragic loss......but in the end the emotions of hope and a lasting love leave the reader knowing.....all will be well.

Kevan Hodges, CEO Ferne Animal Sanctuary

AUTHOR'S NOTE

All books begin their life with a seed of an idea in an author's imagination. This seed could be an event, a character, a scene, a feeling. *The Portrait on the Wall*'s seed was the emotional response I had to Peter Waine's portraits of imaginary pets. I looked at his painting of the parrot I named 'Guy' and thought instantly, 'This is a belle époque parrot who now lives on a houseboat in the Lake District.' I saw the little brown and black dog I called 'Winnie' and knew immediately she was a creation of the Second World War, and then asked myself, 'How on earth could you feed your dog when there was rationing?' I held on to my first thoughts about these pets and then imagined their owners and their unique situations.

It is debatable whether a pet recognises themselves in a painting. They certainly don't ask to be painted. We, loving our pets, value their image, we take photos of them and maybe even commission portraits and drawings of their likeness. As a writer, I was keen to explore this manifestation of love and I had great fun thinking of the different ways a painting can be used in a plot.

Whether you are an animal lover or an art lover, neither, or both, I hope you enjoy *The Portrait on the Wall: Five Special Paintings, Five Cherished Pets*.

Zoë Jasko, 2024

CONTENTS

PACO

PACO

The old man lifted the little girl up to look closely at the painting on the wall. It was a small oil canvas of a terracotta dog with a white bridge to its nose and a white muzzle. Its eyes and nose were as black and shiny as the hair of the little great-granddaughter the old man carried in his arms.

"What is its name, great-grandfather?" the little one asked.

The old man didn't reply. He stayed still, cuddling the child into his chest, looking with elderly eyes at the well-known face of the dog.

"You do remember, don't you, great-grandfather?" she asked anxiously.

"Yes, Conchita, sweetheart, I remember. I remember."

****

Consuelo ran, feet clattering on the old, cobbled stones, away from the wide plaza with the white stone church and along the narrow street which led to the working-class district. Women with woven baskets stood aside to let the bright-eyed child pass, some smiling at her glowing face and flying black locks, others tutting at her lack of decorum.

The street narrowed further as the buildings on either side stretched across the cobbles to meet each other. No doubt they were becoming deaf in their old age and so needed to lean closer to their friend's ear to indulge in the quarter's gossip. Yet bright sunlight from the clear blue sky could still find a way through to touch the high balconies and kiss good morning and good evening to the pots of spring flowers that decorated the sills.

Out of breath, Consuelo arrived at her destination and banged noisily on the heavy wooden door.

"Felipe, he says yes. Papá says yes!" she called out, too impatient to wait for the door to open before announcing her important news.

The door swung open to reveal a boy who was still too narrow for his new height. He smiled broadly at his friend and pulled her, laughing, into his home.

"Consuelo, is it true? Did he agree? What did you do to make him say you could go?" the words tumbled from his mouth, pattering like dry beans spilt on the kitchen table.

"Get me a drink. I'm hot," Consuelo ordered. "Then I will tell you."

A brown earthenware jug, newly filled from the pump, stood on the dresser. Felipe obediently filled a wooden cup while she spoke.

"I ran all the way here. I couldn't wait. Once I've told you, then your Papá will know, and my Papá can't change his mind."

She drank the cool water gratefully, noticing again how shabby Felipe's home was compared to hers. Her jugs were glass, filled by a maid with water from the tap. Her family's rooms drank in the sunshine from the wide balconied windows. Her house boasted a pretty courtyard where vines grew up the walls, and orange trees stood to attention in great ceramic pots. In the centre of her beautiful outside room was a fountain surrounded by expensive blue and white tiles. It was an oasis hidden in the city - a secret place where Consuelo liked to play or read and especially to dance. Felipe's home was small and dark. There was no maid, little sunshine, certainly no pretty courtyard, and no mother.

"I told Papá that your Papá had promised to look after us and not to bring me home late. I also promised to wear my sensible Sunday clothes and not to ask Mamá for a new dress."

That had been a hard promise for her to make. She knew from the servants that all the women and girls wore their best, brightest, festive dresses to the *Feria de Abril de Seville*. Consuelo would have loved to go to the fair in party clothes to match how brightly her heart shone in anticipation. Instead, she would wear a sober black dress and sensible shoes.

"It's alright. You will still look lovely," Felipe reassured her. Ever since he was a tiny boy, he had been in the thrall of the charismatic daughter of his father's old school friend.

"Now, come with me and bring your guitar," Consuelo ordered, leaving the empty cup on the table and heading for the door. "I want to dance."

The friends made their way through the busy streets far from the rich quarter of Consuelo's home and far from the poorer district of Felipe's and crossed Queen Isabella's bridge to the side of the river where they would neither be known nor disturbed. Felipe had picked up his guitar at Consuelo's command. It was an old instrument which had belonged to his father's father, precious to him because of whose it had been and because he could afford no other.

Once Consuelo was satisfied with the spot, Felipe sat down and made music. He played Spanish airs in the classic style, his fingers plucking the strings so they babbled like a brook, he played folk tunes sad and joyful, and when fully warmed up, he experimented with rhythms and melodies of his own. His dark brown eyes were by turns cheerful or thunderous depending on where he felt his heart as he played. Consuelo, for her part, danced to the music Felipe created. She turned and swirled in freedom, free from the niceties of her family and the conformity of the womanhood that awaited her in a future coming closer month by month.

Boats laden with goods passed them, ships from Seville to Cadiz and from Cadiz to Seville. Sailors who noticed the pair waved and smiled. A young lad with olive skin and a serious face watched as he passed on his boat but neither smiled nor waved - only frowned. A dog sat at his feet, alert and expectant, his tongue hanging out, giving the mutt the expression of a smile.

****

The day of the fair arrived. Consuelo felt like a bright hot air balloon; with any more breaths of excitement, she would burst, and if Felipe let go of her hand, she would float away into the sky. Felipe's father had come to her home to collect her, doffing his hat to his old friend, her father.

The *Feria de Abril de Sevilla* - a cattle fair, a festival, a party for the inhabitants of Seville, for the dwellers of the surrounding Andalucían villages and tourists to Spain. Consuelo's heart was in her mouth as she gripped tightly onto Felipe's hand, fearing she might lose him in the thronging streets, jostled and nudged by a hundred people as they approached the entrance to the fair. Posters of a white-dressed lady wrapped in a long pink shawl smiled at Consuelo from every street corner. The beautiful lady, advertising the *Gran Feria de Abril de Sevilla 1910*, seemed to be saying to the excited child, "Come with me, Consuelo. Join us at the fair." Her poster companion, a man, held his guitar so that it pointed towards the fair on the poster horizon, his eyes fixed in the direction of this Spanish celestial city, guiding the white-dressed lady to the festival paradise, just as Felipe held and guided Consuelo.

Carried by the crowd, they arrived before the colossal iron gateway illuminated with nearly eight hundred gas lights, shining like a heavenly beacon, forecasting untold joys on the other side. The crowd pressed forward; women bright in red, yellow, green, and blue dresses tight at the waist and wide at the hip from which cascaded layers and layers of ruffles, bedecked in shawls, from black to white with every colour of the rainbow in between; men in their dark Sunday best suits or dressed to match the bullfight, the *corridas de Toros*.

Felipe's father steered the children through the crowd to a Japanese-style temple covered with paper lanterns and decorated with parasols, where they purchased delicate paper fan mementoes. He took them to admire the prize-winning cattle where the bulls stood proud and where the cows were plump and shining; to the coconut shy, where Felipe struck gold, winning two tough hairy brown coconuts, the stand's plump proprietor stuffing them into a brown paper bag which threatened to tear under its load if not carried carefully by the child's father. He treated them to mounds of pink fluffed candyfloss covering their mouths, cheeks, and hands in sugar as if they had smothered themselves in a cream to soften their skin and sweeten their ecstatic souls.

Consuelo licked her face and fingers with her tongue. She was not at that moment at all elegant. Her mother would have been horrified by her daughter's lack of dignity. But Consuelo threw this thought to the wind. There was only one more thing she wanted to see, one thing so lower-class as to give her mother palpitations - the flamenco.

Felipe's keen ears caught the strains of the *toque*, the guitarist and then all three could hear the *cantaor*, the singer, his baritone voice rising and falling in a *cante chico*, a folk song. Felipe was drawn like a magnet to the source of the sound, dragging Consuelo and his father in his wake, drawn as if his life depended on finding the musicians and hearing them close. A large crowd had gathered around a tent. The crowd was clapping and shouting. Felipe nudged with his elbows and slipped through gaps until he stood, with Consuelo beside him, in the front row of the impromptu audience.

A man in black high-waisted trousers, a black bolero jacket, and a white embroidered shirt was sitting on an upturned wine box, holding his guitar as a beloved creature, absorbed in the melodies his fingers were creating. A second man, the singer, stood close by dressed the same, but his jacket was red. The singer's cheerful song had ended, and now he was taking the audience to a troubled place of sadness, his voice painting a picture of an Andalucía of old.

"Excuse me, Sir, who are they?" Felipe, wide-eyed, asked a thin man with a goatee beard who stood alongside him.

"They are the Rodríguez brothers, Enrique and Ramón, famous throughout Andalucía - and here is their sister Isidra," he said, nodding towards a woman with ebony hair pulled back tight into a bun, who stood several metres from her brothers, almost in the arms of the crowd. Her red satin dress gleamed in the golden evening light, and the ruffles at her calves and ankles flowed like red waves as she stepped slowly and languidly to the rhythms dreamt by her brother's fingers. Around her shoulders, she had tied a black shawl with embroidered red and white silk roses embraced by green silk leaves. Slowly she stepped, shawl tassels swinging, limbs swaying like an almond tree in a gentle summer breeze, raising her arms above her head in graceful *floreo*. The music entered her body through her ears and was carried through her blood to her heart, where she interpreted its meaning in her beautiful limbs. Her sensual movements were silent and hypnotic. Then suddenly, at the very instant that her brothers changed their tone, she cracked the castanets held in an arc over her head and tapped her heels and toes, breaking the reverie.

Consuelo stood entranced. Never had she seen such dancing as Isidra's. Never had she witnessed such authentic flamenco. Occasionally, she had spied snippets of dancing and heard snatches of refrains as she had passed by the city's *Café Cantantes*, the coffee houses with flamenco performances, but she had never been taken to watch or dared to enter alone. She squeezed Felipe's hand to make sure she was not in a dream, and he answered with a squeeze in kind.

A tall youth with olive skin and a furrowed brow watched the children from where he stood among his gypsy kin and scowled. A terracotta dog sat at his feet, his tongue hanging from his mouth in a smile. The mutt's eyes darted from the dancers to the crowd to the dancers. It sat because it had been ordered to by its master, but it was clear for all to see that its passion was with the crowd and the dancers and that at the slightest hint that his master might tolerate his absence, he would be off.

Felipe's father was true to his word and returned Consuelo to her home before the evening was late. She was sticky and dirty but content. Her parents were waiting for her in their pristine drawing room, her mother sitting on a French guilt-lacquered sofa, a book of poems resting on her baby-swollen belly, her father writing at a walnut table nestling in the alcove. He smiled at his daughter,

"So, Consuelo, my treasure, how was the fair?" he asked. "Were the cows worth their prizes?"

"Oh Papá, thank you for letting me go." She ran across the room and jumped onto his welcoming lap, rather too big for that special place but reluctant to give it up.

"Consuelo, you are filthy," her mother commented from her throne. "Alejandro, tell her to wash."

"Candyfloss," he said when he kissed his daughter's cheek, and he winked conspiratorially as he bid her go to her room.

****

"Felipe, I want to dance," Consuelo called from the street to the open window the next day. He grabbed his precious guitar in response and headed with her to the riverside.

"Look, I am Isidra. Watch me dance. You are Ramón." Consuelo held her arms aloft, turning her wrists and stamping her feet. The Seville sun shone warmly on the pair pretending their flamenco to the audience of sailors on the boats passing by.

A tall gypsy lad with olive skin and dark coal eyes was sitting on the grass, whitling a pipe from wood. His terracotta dog lay in the sunshine by his feet. The lad looked up with scorn and called,

"You will never be Isidra. You can never be Ramón."

Consuelo stamped her foot. How dare this peasant speak to her in such a tone!

"You should mind your own business. Nobody asked anything of you," she retorted hotly, and she continued to twirl, ignoring his adolescent rudeness.

The youth stood up from the grass and walked towards Consuelo and Felipe. As if a reflection, the dog got up also, moving closer to the unknown children and sniffing their scents.

"You can never perform the flamenco. You are not gypsy. You will never know how to," the gypsy lad asserted, waving his woodwork in the air in front of their faces for emphasis.

"Teach me then!" The words flew from Consuelo's lips before her brain had considered how to respond, and then for a split second, she wondered if she meant it. This tall stranger was dirty and shabby. He had adolescent spots on his cheeks, and his trousers swung above his ankles. His dark hair was greasy and in a ponytail - a ponytail. What self-respecting young man would wear his hair in that fashion? But what if he knew the secrets of flamenco? She stared at him intently.

"Teach you?" he asked incredulously.

"Yes." She was sure now.

"How old are you?" the stranger asked.

"We are thirteen."

"Too old. Flamenco is an art you grow with."

"How old are you?" she probed.

"Fifteen."

"So old!"

Felipe was watching, anxiously cupping his guitar to his body to keep it safe, but now he reached forward to protect Consuelo from this gypsy stranger and said, "Señor. We love your music, and we do want to learn."

An olive branch had been extended. The youth shrugged in response.

"My name is Bartolo. I have been listening. You don't

play too badly. You seem to have the spirit for your guitar, but her dancing is terrible. I could teach you both, but you will need a *cantaor*, a singer. You are lucky. I like to sing. You must pay me."

Consuelo and Felipe exchanged silent glances. This was strange. This was unexpected. Consuelo could see that Felipe was hesitant but not her. She would take the risk.

"Of course," Consuelo agreed. "Meet us here next week." The bargain was struck.

Bartolo nodded in response but said no more. He turned on his heels and whistled for his dog to follow him. The terracotta mutt turned swiftly, fixed to his master's side, but then changed his mind, returning to the children with his tail wagging and eyes bright, almost as if to leave without saying goodbye was too rude. The white hair on the bridge of his nose and around his muzzle made his black eyes bright and his dark nose shiny. He looked for friendship with enthusiasm, an enthusiasm lacking in his master. Consuelo squatted to the dog's height and rubbed his head and ears with her hands, laughing at the dog's affection and the prospect of real, authentic flamenco lessons with his master.

"Paco!" Bartolo called angrily to his dog. "Come, Paco!"

Paco tore himself away from his new, pretty-smelling friend and trotted happily after his young master.

Consuelo and Felipe returned to the city. As they crossed the Queen Isabella bridge and made their way through the city streets, Felipe wondered how Consuelo would pay Bartolo. He knew she had no money. She had no need.

Whatever she wanted, she was given. He was sure her parents would not pay for dancing lessons with a gypsy boy.

"I have a plan," she assured him, leading him by the hand past the cathedral to the fountain. Silently, they gazed down at the pesetas, strewn wishes, gleaming in the water.

"No, Consuelo, you cannot use these coins to pay Bartolo. This is money for the church," he whispered in disbelief as he began to understand her intentions.

"The church has a lot," she shrugged nonchalantly, and looking around to check that she was not being watched, she dipped her hand into the fountain and fished for pesetas.

"Consuelo!" Felipe was shocked.

"Felipe, it's fine. I promise I will pay the money back to the church in the future. I will remember how many pesetas I have taken, and I will throw it all back in when I am older, more even. I will take it for both of us. This has nothing to do with you. It is between Bartolo and me."

"You and our Lord," he added silently and crossed himself, asking his Saviour in advance for forgiveness.

Bartolo was not a good teacher, at least not at first. Fired by the passion of youth and filled with the flame of the flamenco, he was neither wise nor patient. Their lessons were frequently more filled with shouting than music as Consuelo's own temper quickened. But one thing was true - Bartolo did like to sing. He had a tenor voice that soared into the blue sky like a wintering swallow, a voice that could tell any story, live any feeling. Paco, too seemed to enjoy the lessons. When the tempo was fast, the key a lively major, he would race from performer to performer, bounding excitedly to each, as if joining in the happy dance. When the tempo was slow, the key a sad minor, he would sit at Bartolo's feet until Consuelo began to dance, whereupon he would lift himself to follow her steps as dismally as any scorned lover.

"Why do we never have our lessons where you live, Bartolo?" Consuelo asked one day as the three, worn from their practice, lazed for a moment on the bank by the riverside and as she caressed the skin beneath the terracotta dog's wiry hair.

"Here is as good a place as any," Bartolo replied.

"But I would like to see your home," she said and then, seeing that her request had not produced the desired response, she commanded, "Take me to your home, Bartolo!"

Felipe sat up anxiously. He was used now to mediating between his hot-headed friends. How was it, he wondered, that Consuelo could not see that Bartolo keenly felt the difference in their backgrounds? Felipe knew that the quarters of the city society that separated him from Consuelo were far apart, but from Consuelo's Plaza to Bartolo's gypsy camp, the social distance was ever further.

Bartolo did not answer her.

"Paco!" he called to his dog. "Come here, Paco!"

Paco obediently left Consuelo's caresses and went to his master.

"I'll think about it, Consuelo," Bartolo said as he stood up to leave with Paco.

"Are we finished for today?" Consuelo asked. "I thought we were going to dance one last song?"

"I've had enough for today," Bartolo called over his shoulder.

"Will you think about it then?"

"Yes, Consuelo, I will."

Bartolo left his two friends by the side of the river.

"How could she come back with us?" he said softly to his dog as he hastened to his home.

Consuelo made him angry. She had everything - privilege, wealth, beauty. She carried the knowledge of entitlement on her skin; she wore it as a lens in her eyes. He had seen this from the first moment he had seen her on the boat as she danced by the river, and in the crowd at the *Feria de Abril de Seville,* when they were all, as yet, unknown to each other.

Yet he admired her. He admired her for her pride, for her passion to learn his gypsy culture, and for her determination to succeed. He wished he could say this to her. He wished he could have the easy rapport with her that she had with his dog. If he were Paco, Consuelo would touch him, would stroke him. His heart leapt as he thought it. Quickly, he smothered the sparks of his desire. Consuelo would never like him more than his dog.

"Paco!" he called angrily, even though the dog trotted

obediently beside him. "Paco, home!" and he scowled as the terracotta dog shot ahead of him as if his command had been a gun, racing to beat his master to the gypsy camp on the outskirts of the city.

No more was said of visiting the gypsy camp, and soon Consuelo's attention was diverted by the arrival of her mother's longed-for baby, a boy - Roberto. Baby cuddles and toddler games in the beautiful courtyard vied for time alongside her obvious studies and her clandestine dancing.

The seasons turned, and the children grew. Almost without noticing, their teenage years were on the cusp of being left behind forever. In the time that had passed, Bartolo, Felipe and Consuelo had mellowed, or at least softened at the edges, growing together slowly in the direction of a real flamenco trio. Bartolo and Felipe were no longer boys. They were now handsome young Spaniards with men's voices and shaven chins, and Consuelo was a woman as curvaceous and lithe as the sound of her name. Bartolo was pleased with Felipe's progress. Although he knew nothing of the suffering of exclusion that was the inheritance of the Spanish gypsies, Felipe still absorbed and breathed the gypsy airs, which he blended with the ancient Jewish melodies and the Moorish rhythms of his own inheritance, filtering them through the sadness in his life to make haunting flamenco guitar. Yes, Felipe was mastering the *palos*, the musical styles, and could match Bartolo's skill as the *cantaor*. But Consuelo, Bartolo frowned as he thought of her, she knew the steps, she had mastered the moves, but she was acting, she was not feeling.

"Consuelo, you must feel the *duende*. You must live the

mood of the dance," Bartolo would criticize her.

"I am!" she would shout in return. "Look how sad my face is when I must be sad."

"That is not real sadness," he scoffed. "You must dance passion. You must dance love. You must dance loss."

"How can I dance what I do not know?" eighteen-year-old Consuelo grumbled to Felipe as he accompanied her home to her fine house on the Plaza. And then she was struck with a new thought,

"Felipe, how can you do what Bartolo wants with the music?" she asked, turning to look at her childhood friend, and, as she did, she saw the man he had become for the first time. In her confusion, she blushed.

"I don't know, Consuelo," he replied thoughtfully. "I think it starts with this." He took his guitar to his chest in a loving embrace. "I remember my grandfather. He used to play all day - morning, evening, mealtimes even. I would wake up to the music and fall asleep to it too. When my mother died, he stopped playing and soon after that, he stopped living. When Bartolo takes the flamenco to where it is sad, I think of my grandfather and my mother, and the melodies just come into my fingers. And when the music is happy, I think of waking up to my grandfather playing and my mother smiling, and I think of you and me, Consuelo, by the river when we were small."

As a child, Consuelo would have taken Felipe's hand as he spoke, but as a young woman, she felt strangely embarrassed. His words awoke a sadness in her heart that she had not felt before. If Felipe had had the words to explain his loss and his longing years earlier, she would have reached out in friendship but not in understanding. She was no longer a little girl, and he was no longer a little boy. They could never again be as they were. She realised that she too now felt an ache of loss for that time which could never be recovered, and in some small way, she could now catch a glimpse of Felipe's loss - the loss of people he had loved and who had loved him. She had never truly understood loss and sadness until that moment as they walked together through the streets of Old Seville.

She made her way home in unusual silence. The late autumn day was still warm, and the swelling oranges on the trees were beginning to ripen. Soon they would be bright globes, miniature suns resplendent amid the dark evergreen leaves and then they would be harvested. Townsfolk would join together to pick the succulent sweet-smelling Seville oranges, and the aroma of the fresh fruit would perfume the air of each district of the city and float into every home. Rich and poor would become equal in the gift bestowed by the trees that lined the boulevards and hid in the courtyards. She spent the afternoon quietly pretending to read while watching Roberto play with his nurse. It would not be long, she thought sadly, before her parents noticed that she was too old to be alone with her childhood friend Felipe and she would lose her companion and her dancing in one stroke. She ached at the thought and wished she could be five years old, like Roberto, all over again.

The next day as she danced, Bartolo neither shouted nor sang. He watched, and he listened, and at the end of his lesson, he said,

"There will be a party tonight at the camp. There will be dancing. You should come."

Felipe and Consuelo looked at each other in disbelief. Was Bartolo finally inviting them to his home after all this time?

"Well, you don't have to come," Bartolo added, on an unsure footing, when he found that the invitation he was so casually giving, the invitation which he knew was so keenly sought, was not immediately accepted.

"Thank you," Consuelo replied hastily. "We will come."

Felipe caught Consuelo's attention with a light touch on her arm.

"How, Consuelo? How will you be allowed out at night?" he whispered.

She thought for a moment and replied,

"I will send a message that I am staying to dine with you and that you will walk me home later."

"But what will your parents think, Consuelo? You have never dined with us in the evening."

"I don't care what my parents think. I want to go to the gypsy camp," she cried, pulling away from her friend. She walked gracefully, unaware of the sensual movement of her limbs, to Bartolo and linked her arm through his.

"What will it be like tonight at your camp?" she asked him, bright-eyed and expectant, as she began to walk along the riverside path with him, leaving Felipe and Paco on the grass behind.

The camp's fire burnt bright that night, and the music was joyful. Felipe had expected, as city folk, that they would be greeted with suspicion by Bartolo's gypsy kin, but he had been wrong. They were offered food and friendship. He had brought his guitar with him, and both he and his instrument were welcomed. Bartolo's uncle invited him warmly to sit alongside him and play, which he did for hour after hour until the night was cold and the campfire low.

Bartolo introduced Consuelo to his grandmother and his aunts. His cousins took her merrily by the hand and showed her the camp while he hung back with the menfolk. The girls showed her the caravans, dark green, made darker by the pitch of the night, covered with depictions of flowers that would have been bright in the daylight but which were mysterious knots in the flickering yellow firelight.

Paco followed Consuelo and guarded her jealously. Although the maidens of the camp were his friends, the sweet-smelling Consuelo was his chosen one, and he wanted no other person nor beast to take possession of her. He need not have worried. The beasts of the camp paid her no attention. The horses stabled in the paddock nearby were quiet shadows, occasionally whinnying and the sounds of their breath and their hooves on the grass were hidden by the music and song around the campfire. Dogs, whose masters were Bartolo's kin, rested under the caravans. A grey kitten slept in the lap of a sleeping child, in the arms of a sleeping grandfather. All three had been left on a bench by the wakeful ones to enjoy the party in their slumber.

Far from the fire and close to the caravans, a gypsy artist had set up an easel and was painting. Canvasses he had already finished that night stood upright to attention, drying, leaning against the wheels of his home. Consuelo moved closer to look.

On his easel was the form of a flamenco dancer, one arm raised in an arc above her head, the other lifting her skirts to step and to dance.

"What colour will she be?" Consuelo asked.

"What colour would you like, young friend?" he replied.

"Red," she answered, remembering Isidra Rodríguez at the April fair.

"Red, she shall be then, young friend."

"No, wait," she interrupted.

"Gold. Let her be dressed in cream and gold."

Consuelo turned to look at the paintings drying by the caravan. Each one was of a flamenco dancer, all women, swaying, twisting, turning to inaudible, invisible music, all dressed in bright colours, but none in cream and gold.

"Why have you painted so many dancers?" she asked.

"Because they are beautiful," he replied.

"Is that so?"

He laughed.

"You are a clever young one," he replied. "Because they will sell and make me money."

He put down his paintbrush and palette, laying them at the foot of the easel like an offering on an altar to a god. He took a packet of tobacco and a piece of thin white paper from his pocket and expertly rolled himself a cigarette, which he lit with a match from a box in his other pocket. As he did so, the artist scarcely took his eyes off her. She was like no other young woman he had ever seen. She had a presence. She met and held his gaze like none of his own kind could. After drawing twice on his newly rolled cigarette, he asked,

"Would you like me to paint you, young friend?"

"Yes," she thought, "I would like to be painted, but not now, not as I am."

Paco, impatient to return to the campfire activity from where he could smell tasty meat skewers roasting, pushed against her leg and then pointed his nose in the direction of the fire, wagging his tail, making it clear to her where he wanted them to head.

"Thank you," she answered the painter. "It is very kind of you to offer. Do you paint animals? Could you paint my dog?"

He looked quizzically at her before lowering his eyes to a camp mutt he had rarely considered.

"Yes, young friend, I could paint Bartolo's dog for you."

"Thank you," she smiled sweetly before following Paco to the food at the campfire.

After eating, they danced. They danced and danced. Consuelo swirled and twirled with her new friends - finding their rhythm - glimpsing their souls.

February came, and the streets of Seville were filled with the perfume of thousands of orange trees in bloom as millions of creamy stars covered the dark green trees. Consuelo's father, Alejandro, was reading his newspaper one morning, sitting at his walnut table in his drawing room.

"It says here, my love, that the King and Queen will be coming to the April fair," he commented to his wife, who sat embroidering next to the long window that overlooked their courtyard. "I think maybe it is time that we all attended, even little Roberto. He is old enough now to join us." And before Josefina could object, he added, "I think perhaps a new dress for you, my love, and Consuelo. I believe a certain style is worn to the fair, even by ladies of our class. We will travel there by motorcar, of course."

Consuelo trembled with excitement when she learnt of her father's plan. What if, just what if, she could dance with Bartolo and Felipe at the fair as she had seen Isidra Rodríguez dance to the music of her brothers, Enrique, and Ramón, all those years before? The thought stole her breath.

"You are mad, Consuelo," was Bartolo's unfettered response when she told him what she wanted.

"But Bartolo, we can meet by the tents. We will choose a spot, Felipe will begin to play and you to sing, the crowd will make space, and I will dance."

"No!" he spat, his deep frown returning as afore to his brow.

"What is it, Bartolo? Are we not good enough? Or are

we not gypsy enough?"

He squirmed before her challenging, angry gaze, her discomforting passion.

"No, you are good enough - now."

"Consuelo," Felipe added quietly. "Your parents will be angry. They will not want to see their daughter dance with people like us at the cattle fair. Not where their friends might be, not where the King and Queen will be."

"But don't you see?" Consuelo begged, hot tears stinging her eyes, "This could be my only chance, my last. Please."

Bartolo shrugged, dug his hands deep into his pockets, and turned away.

"Bartolo?" Felipe called gently after him. The gypsy lad paused and called over his shoulder,

"You will need a new dress Consuelo, not a black dress for Mass, and not something your mother would choose. I will speak to my *abuela*." And then he was off, leaving Consuelo to exhale a small sigh of relief and Felipe to doubt the wisdom of the plan.

The image of Consuelo in a tight-fitting flamenco dress excited him. He yearned to see her dressed in the fantasy they shared. He understood the risk they would be running. He knew, deep down, that it would be one moment, one single moment in their lives, and that the moment of Consuelo's dance at the fair must be perfect. She must be perfect.

Bartolo's grandmother was not as old as her raisin-wrinkled skin suggested. Her life had been hard. When a child, she had travelled with her parents and siblings through the towns and villages of Andalucía, fruit-picking, and harvesting, wandering from village to village, her father finding labour with farmers, blacksmiths, and farriers. As gypsy-folk, they had been regarded with either suspicion or tolerant indifference. She had borne fourteen children, ten surviving to adulthood. Now she lived in the gypsy camp beyond the poorest outlying district of Seville, where her husband had brought her and their brood when he found work in the ceramic factory many years ago. Bartolo had often spoken to her about Felipe and Consuelo, and she had grinned secretly at the thought of her tall, proud grandson so deeply attached to the ways of his gypsy heritage and yet learning to live and work with non-gypsies, indeed, to become their friends. She had been impressed by the two young city-dwellers when they visited the camp the night of their party. Consuelo and Felipe had left city prejudice at the city's gates. They had arrived open and innocent as children to join the festivities and, as a result, had been welcomed into the large gypsy family's bosom.

"*Abuela*," Bartolo said, "Consuelo needs a dress for her flamenco. Her own dresses will not do."

His grandmother chuckled silently; how sure youth was that he was right!

"Darling *Abuela*," he coaxed, kissing her dark papery cheek. "Don't you have a dress from the aunts in your trunk?"

"My fine young man," she replied, taking her grandson's

hand. "Of course, I have dresses in my trunk. But they are not for your friend."

He frowned at her reply and was set to coax more when she added,

"Every flamenco dance is the dancer's story, the dancer's reply to your voice, Bartolo, and to the guitarist's strings. She can wear no dress but her own. Otherwise, she is only pretending. The dresses in my trunk are old. They are not for a girl who is scarcely nineteen. They are the dresses of your aunts' youth, not of Consuelo's."

Holy Week was approaching, and the fair was only two weeks away on the other side. Consuelo's mother would also visit the fair for the first time. King Alfonso VIII and Queen Victoria Eugenia would be in attendance. The fair was now a 'society' event to be seen at, not a lower-class melée to be avoided. Josefina and all her friends were caught up in the excitement. New dresses had been agreed upon, and a famous couturier had visited the large house on the Plaza.

Josefina had fussed with the fashion plates that the couturier had brought with her. Fashions from Madrid, Paris, New York, and London - the artists' impressions of smiling young women showing off the new styles overwhelmed her. How much more straightforward for Consuelo to wear a simple dark dress like the one she was going to wear, despite her husband's suggestions that she try something different. Consuelo, however, pored with the couturier over the dress designs, secretly considering which might be modest enough to please her parents, sensual enough to please Bartolo and perfect enough to please herself.

The dresses arrived packed with tissue paper into strong card boxes hand-painted with almond leaves and almond flowers, the signature of the famous couturier. Consuelo's stomach tingled with flying butterflies as she opened the lid and saw her dress waiting for her. Her maid whisked it away before she could touch it and play with the beautiful fabric, hanging both garments up in Josefina's wardrobe to wait for their special day.

In a blink of an eye, it was time for the *Feria de Abril de Sevilla*. Consuelo was sure it was more exciting than any of the Feasts of Three Kings that she could remember. Her maid helped her dress that evening in front of the long, gilt-edged mirror that hung on the wall of her bedroom. The dress was beautiful. It was perfect. It was such a deep cream, almost to be the palest of yellows. It had a soft lace bodice and loose lace sleeves that reached almost, but not quite, to the elbow. Three deep panels of lace formed the skirt, the first finishing just below her hips, the second extending to her calves and the lowest reaching her ankles - a waterfall of innocent ruffles. Consuelo's modesty could not be questioned in this dress. But the dress was also rebellious, for a gold silk sleeveless tunic was placed over the top creating a deep cream V-shape over her breasts from the fabric of the dress below. A gold sash held the tunic in place, with a cheeky tie at the waist before it dangled flamboyantly to the ground. Turquoise panels rose on the tunic from her waist to her shoulders, and onto the panels, clusters of tiny orange blossoms had been embroidered by hand. The maid drew Consuelo's thick black hair tight over her head and wove her hair into plaits, pinning them up with silk orange blossoms and a white comb to complete the ensemble.

"Consuelo, my treasure, you are a delight," her father admired as his daughter entered the hall where her parents were waiting for her, ready to depart. Little Roberto, holding his mother's hand, was already pulling her towards the door, anxious that they step into the street without delay and mount the amazing invention - his father's motorcar, a contraption that delighted his soon-to-be six-year-old soul as much as thoughts of the fair.

"Ahem," Alejandro coughed, slightly embarrassed. "Consuelo, my sweet, your couturier told me that this is the height of fashion." He signalled for the parlour maid to come forward with a rectangular box covered in hand-painted almond blossom and leaves. "And I decided you should have it, my treasure, even though it will give your mother palpitations."

In the box was a gorgeous, extravagant fan made from ostrich feathers dyed an orange-gold to compliment the dress.

"Your mother would have preferred the feathers to be white to match your beautiful dress, but, my treasure, I sometimes think it is worth taking a risk in life."

"Thank you, Papá, thank you!" Consuelo exclaimed joyously, but she trembled at the thought of the risk she would soon take and the fear that her father might not be quite so proud of her then. She buried that thought as quickly as she could.

The fair was wonderful. Wide-eyed Roberto could not be budged from the entrance gate, which, covered in hundreds of bright lights shining like stars in a galaxy, rooted his little legs to the spot until Consuelo's description of candy floss enticed him over the threshold. Alejandro wanted to see the cattle. In truth, he had wanted to attend the fair for many years, but his wife's disinterest had deterred him. Caught up in the enthusiasm and the gaiety of the people of Seville enjoying their fair, he resolved to make the treat an annual event. Josefina, however, clung to her husband's arm, nervous and worried by the presence of so many common people.

Consuelo tried hard to enjoy herself, but with every step she took deeper into the fairground, she felt more and more sick and fearful. What a fool she had been to want to dance the flamenco in front of all these people. All too soon, the family had reached the tents, and Consuelo saw her friends waiting for her. Felipe was sitting on an upturned box, holding his guitar close to his chest, anxiously scanning the crowd, looking for her. Bartolo, meanwhile, lurked close to the tents, his hands thrust deep into his pockets, scowling. Despite the deep frown, he was handsome, oh so handsome, in dark trousers, a white shirt and red brocade waistcoat. Paco was close by, as usual, and was sniffing the canvas backs of the nearby stalls, pausing to eye the crowd before sniffing again.

Bartolo did not recognise his city friend at first, so changed was she from a girl to a young lady. He could not hide his admiration for her beneath a scowl. It broke out and transformed his features. She was pleased to see him and pleased at his response.

Felipe noticed her next. The three exchanged glances, the signal that they were ready. Then gently, softly, Felipe began to play. The music spread like a waft of perfume over those standing nearby. They stopped their conversations and started listening to the young man playing on an upturned box. As more began to listen, Bartolo moved closer to Felipe and added his voice to the guitar. It was a popular folk song that many knew. The crowd increased, and men clapped and cheered. Paco, too barked his appreciation. Josefina was alarmed by the building crowd and anxiously started to direct the family away from the tents, but Consuelo was determined to stay. She pulled away from her mother and discreetly took up her intended position in the front row of the audience, where a stage space had now formed in front of her friends.

The *palos* changed. Felipe was taking Bartolo, Consuelo, and the audience with him to a new place, away from the familiar folk song and to an imagined place of expectancy. The slow rhythm entered Consuelo's feet, and with the next beat, she stepped onto the stage arching her back elegantly as she raised her arms high and paused, keeping the audience anticipating her next move, only to unexpectedly twist around at the next beat - lace tiers ruffling, golden silk gleaming. Then, spiralling her arms and her wrists, she flicked open her golden feather fan with a flourish before turning into the arms of the waiting Bartolo. With an answering flamenco *floreo* of his wrists, he silently, sensually presented her with a pair of castanets which she accepted with a *pasa doble* bow before turning again to hold the eyes of the crowd and her astonished parents in her proud gaze. A pulse of electricity seemed to pass over the three friends; in an instant, the *palos* changed again to fast and furious. Consuelo tapped and twirled, she arched and grew as their flamenco performance told the story of Bartolo's fight for inclusion, of Felipe's loss and of her own need for freedom. She was Isidra Rodríguez. She was Consuelo - for an instant, only an instant, before her furious father dragged her by the wrist from the improvised stage space through the thronging crowd, followed by her mother crying and Roberto howling, to their motorcar.

"Consuelo, how could you? How could you create such an exhibition of yourself in front of the whole of Seville? The King and Queen could have seen you!" Her mother cried angrily from the safety of the motorcar, out of earshot from all but the family. "We will never live this down. You are no daughter of mine!"

Her father, meanwhile, gripped the steering wheel in silence, his anger making a gargoyle of his features.

"Risk is one thing, young lady," he said on the steel edge of his voice. "Ridicule is quite another."

At first, when his beautiful daughter had caught the rhythm of the music and stepped into the performance space, he, like the crowd, had been held captive by the moment, unable and unwilling to take his eyes off her. The spell had been broken by Josephina's insistent tugging on his sleeve. For the first time, he understood that his daughter was a woman who could express her sexuality in movement in front of hundreds of admiring eyes, and he had to remove her from that gaze.

Consuelo sat in the back of the car in utter stillness. Their words hurt her, and their expressions wounded her, but the music of the flamenco in her head and the muscle memory of the dance in her limbs comforted her. Their duet of punishments for her behaviour rumbled around her in the car as the car's wheels rumbled on the road.

Not long later, Consuelo ran on the cobbled stones in the stillness of the midnight city, the light touch of her step the only sound. Clutching her bag, she ran past the cathedral and over the Queen Isabella bridge; only then did she slacken her pace to a walk, but it was not a measured one. She made swift strides along the bank of the river out of the city to the gypsy camp. She paused at the camp's edge and scrutinised the sleeping caravans. In which one was Bartolo? She could not remember. She was unsure she had been shown it on the night of the gypsy party. Slithers of smoke rose from the dying fire that would have burnt bright only a few hours ago.

She had an idea.

"Paco," she called. "Paco," and then she whistled in imitation of the dog's master.

There was no response from the dog.

She crept a little further into the camp. She felt like a trespasser now that she was an uninvited guest. For a moment, her usual certainty wavered.

"Paco," she called again, "Paco, please come. I need Bartolo," she whispered.

She waited and was on the verge of leaving with a heavy heart, her task unfulfilled, when the terracotta dog emerged sleepily from under a caravan at the edge of the camp and made his way, questioningly, towards her.

She dropped her travel bag at her feet and squatted down to greet Paco, rubbing his ears and neck with her hands and nuzzling her face into his flank.

"Oh, Paco, I'm so glad I've found you," she said gently.

Then she stood up, tall and straight, full of authority.

"Where is Bartolo, Paco? Take me to Bartolo," she commanded.

The dog, recognising his master's name and his beloved Consuelo's command, turned his head toward the caravan where he had been sleeping and barked.

"Sshh, Paco," she said quickly. "We don't want anyone to hear us. Is it that one, is it?"

He bounded to the caravan in response and began to paw at the door, whining softly as he did so. Consuelo followed and stood behind him, waiting.

"Paco, be quiet!" she heard Bartolo grumble, "I'm sleeping."

"Bartolo," she then called softly through the closed door of the caravan. "Bartolo, it's me, Consuelo."

"Consuelo?" she heard him reply in confusion.

What in God's name was Consuelo doing outside his caravan in the dead of night? He thought to himself. Was he dreaming? Goodness knows he had dreamt enough of her coming to him. He lit the candle next to his bed with a match, then fumbled to dress, hastily pulling on a shirt and stepping into his trousers.

He opened the door and saw her, pale-faced and strained, her hand resting on his dog's head, her travel bag at her feet.

"Consuelo, are you alright?" he asked worriedly.

"I wouldn't be here if I were alright," she answered, true to her usual argumentative form.

"You'd better come in," he said, holding the door open for her. Paco pushed past their legs and entered.

They looked out into the darkness of the camp from the step of his caravan, instinctively checking that no one had seen her arrive, that no one had seen her enter.

The candle lit the bed and the small table it stood on but left the recesses of the caravan in darkness. Bartolo took Consuelo by the hand, led her to the bed, and sat with her on its edge, still holding her hand. She did not release hers from his.

"Why have you come, Consuelo?" he asked softly.

For a moment, she didn't know. For a moment, all she could register was the feeling of her hand in his, the amber softness of the flesh on his chest where he had not done up the buttons of his shirt, the musk of his nighttime sweat. She felt dizzy. Not the dizziness that she loved, the dancing, twirling dizziness of the flamenco. The dizziness of something unexpected, unlooked for, unwanted. She pulled her hand away from Bartolo's and said coolly,

"I've come to say goodbye, Bartolo."

"Goodbye?" He was stunned. He had not been expecting Consuelo to come to his caravan tonight, and now that she was here, he was not expecting her to say goodbye.

"Why goodbye? Where are you going?"

"I cannot stay. I cannot live the way my parents expect me to live. They have forbidden me to see Felipe. They have forbidden me to see you. They have forbidden me to dance. They have forbidden me to live!" she proclaimed with the full authority and calamity of youth.

"Don't be ridiculous, Consuelo. You cannot go."

"How dare you tell me what I can and cannot do," she retorted in full voice. Her face, which seconds earlier had been pale, became flushed with colour as her temper began to flare, as it so frequently did in Bartolo's presence.

"Sssh," he hushed. "Someone will hear us." He reached for her hand again, and she let him hold it.

"Where will you go?" he asked gently.

"To Madrid."

He had so many questions. What would she do there? How would she live? But his lips could form only one.

"Who will go with you?" he probed, fearing the answer.

"No one," she replied. "I will go alone."

He breathed an inaudible sigh of relief. She was not fleeing with Felipe, then.

"Does Felipe know?" he asked.

"No. I haven't told him. I came here to say goodbye to you. I want you to say goodbye to Felipe for me."

"Consuelo!" Bartolo rebuked her. "I can't do that. You can't expect me to say goodbye to him for you. He's your oldest friend. He's like your brother."

"I know," she said sadly. "Which is why I can't tell him. You must."

She held his gaze as she spoke. Her eyes were as much filled with remorse as challenge.

"Bartolo?" she said.

"Yes."

"You want to kiss me, don't you?"

"Yes!" he replied, surprised, unsure of what was about to happen, what the strange and enchanting Consuelo expected.

"You may kiss me then," she said, raising her mouth to greet his and to kiss him for what she knew would be both the first and the last time.

They kissed in the candlelight, on the bed in the gypsy caravan and then she drew away and prepared to leave.

"Goodbye, Bartolo."

"Don't go," he begged her.

"I must," she replied, tears beginning to sting her eyes.

"Well, at least don't go alone."

"I must," the girl repeated.

"Take Paco with you. He will look after you. He will protect you."

Hearing his name, Paco, who had been lying by the door, waiting for the two he loved to finish whatever they were doing on the bed, raised his head in question.

"I can't take Paco with me. He's your dog," she gasped.

Hearing his name for a second time, Paco got up and padded to Consuelo, where he buried his head into her lap, absorbing the scratch tickles and caresses she scattered over his crown and shoulders.

"You must," Bartolo asserted gently.

"Thank you," she replied with a true and grateful heart.

He held the door open for the young woman he loved and her dog to leave him and step out into the unknown of the night. On its threshold, she turned and kissed him again, her resolve to leave almost failing her. At length, she pulled away from Bartolo and left with no more words and without looking back.

He couldn't bear to watch them disappear into the night, so he shut the caravan door to obscure their departure. Going over to the bedside table, he picked up his candle, raised it to the gloom of the wall above, and let its light shine on two small paintings hanging side by side. On the left, a terracotta dog with a white muzzle, and on the right, a girl dressed in cream and gold, dancing.

"Goodbye, Consuelo. Goodbye, Paco," he said gently, blowing out his candle and climbing, fully dressed, into bed, where he found no sleep until the morning.

When he woke, late in the day, he paid no heed to his crumpled state. He took the painting of the dancing girl down from its place on his caravan wall and hurried to Felipe's house. The news of Consuelo's departure had already reached him. Her distraught father had visited in the early morning, demanding to be told what he knew of his daughter's flight and leaving the lad in despair.

"She wanted you to have this," Bartolo lied to Felipe, handing him her dancing portrait. "My uncle painted it after the party," he explained. "But she told me last night that she wanted you to have it." His words and tone were casual, as if the painting meant nothing to either of them.

Felipe let his tears flow unabashed as he took the painting of the swirling Consuelo doing what she loved best - dancing.

"It's kind of her, but don't you want it?" he asked. He was not blind to the feelings he knew Bartolo hid behind his pretend indifference.

"I don't need it," Bartolo said. "I have Paco."

"Paco?"

"Yes, uncle painted Paco too, as she asked, but we never had the chance to give the paintings to her," Bartolo lied again. When his uncle had finished the paintings, Bartolo had not been able to bring himself to give them to Consuelo. He had had a vague sense that by keeping the pictures in his cabin, he was somehow keeping hold of Consuelo. But now she was gone. Keeping the paintings for himself had not kept her. He knew that Felipe loved her too. Whether as a brother or as a lover, he did not know and did not care to explore. There were two paintings, and there were two men. It was only right they should have one each, and as he could not bear to bring his eyes to the swirling, twirling cream and gold dancer on the canvas, he had given it to Felipe.

"Whenever I look at the painting of Paco, I will think of him and her." And now he spoke the truth.

There was so much more the two young men could have said but didn't. They could have admitted how much they both loved her, how worried they were for her safety and how they feared they would never see her again. Not yet twenty-one years of age, Bartolo left Felipe's home feeling like an old man and returned to the gypsy camp and his work on the boats.

****

Years later, a very old man, he held his little great-granddaughter up to look at the painting of a terracotta dog which now hung on the wall of his house, not his caravan.

"What's the dog's name, great-grandfather?" she asked.

"Paco, my Conchita. No, wait - Consuelo."

"Great-grandfather, it can't be both," she said earnestly, a mini adult rebuking an old man for incorrect information.

"Paco. Consuelo. I hardly remember now. I look at Paco and see Consuelo. I think of Consuelo, and I look at Paco."

"Great-grandfather, you are silly," the little girl said, wriggling down from his arms. "Come into the garden now and watch me dance," she insisted, taking old Bartolo by the hand and urging him out into the Seville spring sunshine filled with the aroma of orange blossom.

GUY

At war with the world, a young man set out from his new lodgings at the white-fronted Belle Vue boarding house on Lake Street and marched with purpose down the lane leading to the water's edge. He wore a light flannel suit, and a newly bought brown leather satchel strung across his chest, which bounced uncomfortably on his hip at each angry stride he took. He looked neither left nor right as he made for the lake, disinterested in the shop and hotel fronts along the way. When he arrived at Keswick's pleasure gardens, nothing could could catch his attention and deter him from his goal of reaching the Derwent Water shore, not even the heavy scent of the mauve lilac bushes or the buttery buds of the early yellow roses.

A young lady in a blue dress, out for a walk with her Mama, turned to look at him when he passed; but he did not see. All he could see was Valerie. Valerie Pearson, who had taken his heart, broken it into a thousand pieces, a million even, and thrown the crumbs of his life's muscle to the ducks in the Serpentine Pond in Hyde Park. He would have given every ounce of himself to please Valerie. He would have travelled around the world with her, bearing her luggage and attending to her every whim. Hell! He would have even housed, fed and watered the bloody ducks on the Serpentine in Hyde Park if she had indicated that would have pleased her. The young lady in blue turned to her mother, who shrugged in upper-class charm.

"Riff Raff in a suit, Mathilda," the Mama commented,

and the two continued their way from the water's edge to the tea-room in the town.

The 'Riff Raff' reached the rim of Derwent Water and threw himself down onto a vacant bench with a sigh loud enough to indicate to a couple of passers-by that he should be left alone and that they should not seek to share occupancy of the bench. He need not have worried. The two gentlemen had taken one look at the young man's thunderous expression and decided that they should steer well clear of him.

The view from the bench was, by chance, well-chosen. It had been positioned flush to the quayside wall, and from it, almost the entire expanse of the lake could be seen. It made the young man feel like he was sitting at the edge of a picture, up close against the frame. In front of him was a small jetty with a handful of rowing boats available to hire. However, there did not seem to be anyone in sight whose job it was to take the money from the few holiday makers who had ventured into Cumbria so early in the season. A family of ducks floated on the water close to the boats. He scowled at them. They had better not come close if they knew what was good for them.

Not wishing to dwell on the ducks, he raised his eyes and took in the full view before him. The shore directly opposite could not be that far away, he thought. It would not take much effort to row to the other side. The lake curled around to his right to become obscured by the small town of Keswick. When it came back into view, he could see a pretty marina on the north side, where sailing boats, rowing boats, and even a houseboat were moored. Derwent Water extended far beyond him to his left, the lie of the land preventing him from observing its southern tip. He knew that the lake was not large. The path around it would be no more than ten miles long. He might explore it one day this summer if he could summon the energy and the enthusiasm.

Looking now into the middle of the lake, he could see a large island crowned with an elegant cream house. Scattered nearby were several other islands, some scarcely more than a collection of boulders. There was little activity on the lake that morning; to his right, a boat with a bright white sail made its way southbound and approaching the furthest island, he could make out a rowing boat with two indistinguishable passengers aboard.

The slight wind that aided the sailing boat on its way also licked the young man's floppy straw hair, as if that were a sail. He shivered slightly. It was foolish to think that May was summer. He opened his satchel and took out a sketch book. The name Freddie Booth decorated the front cover in the curls and swirls of artistic Victorian copper plate, letters designed by that young man when he had intended to sketch but when nothing other than his name had captured his imagination.

He flicked through the book to a blank page, a white space ready for an artistic attempt. Taking a graphite pencil from his satchel, he attacked the page with lines the same way he had attacked the path from his lodgings to the shore. If he gave himself time to think, he wouldn't do it. He wouldn't draw because he would never find the resolve to start. This was how he found he was sketching the boats' outlines in the opposite marina. He stabbed lines on the paper, hastily cutting into the fresh white. As the grey forms began appearing, Freddie settled into a rhythm and became calmer, now taking time to observe, slowing his effort to shade carefully and bring out the nuances he felt and saw. Almost without conscious effort, the Nichol End marina, its sailing boats, its rowing boat, and its houseboat appeared as a sketch before his eyes. He was pleased with his effort and that, for a short time, Valerie Pearson had been banished from his thoughts.

The day that Freddie chose to walk around Derwent Water, a fortnight later, was fresh and sunny.

"Ah, you will enjoy that, Mr Booth, indeed you will," Mr Maddison, the proprietor of the Belle Vue boarding house, commented when Freddie had reported his plans for the day at breakfast.

"Will you stop to paint on your way round, Mr Booth?"

"No, not today, Mr Maddison, it's too much bother to carry my paints. I think I'll merely sketch the views which take my fancy and return to paint later in the summer."

Freddie spoke these words at a measured pace. Mr Maddison was pleased. When the lad had arrived at the beginning of the month, he had only spoken when spoken to, and when he did respond to a question, he was a dog biting off one's hand. Mr Maddison had been warned as much in the letter Freddie's parents had sent securing the summer accommodation for their angry son nursing a broken heart.

Mr Maddison paused briefly before adding, "Ruskin

used to paint around here. Some say his work was rather good."

"Probably," the young man responded with an air of indifference. "Not my style though, too old-fashioned."

"We don't have that many gentlemen artists that come here," Mr Maddison continued, enjoying conversation with the lad, which was now rolling. "It tends to be more the young ladies with their water colours that paint the countryside. They don't go much up to the hills, though. It's the young men that do that. You'd like the peaks, Mr Booth. You could paint up there one day, perhaps."

"Maybe I shall," Freddie acknowledged. "But today, my sketchbook will be filled with views of the lake from all sides." For a second, Freddie smiled, and his face became handsome and pleasantly roguish.

Mr Maddison seemed to be hardly listening.

"Now writers, Mr Booth," the boarding house proprietor added. "There seem to be a lot of writers who come here nowadays - sometimes for a few weeks on their holidays, sometimes for the whole season. There's a writer who lives on his houseboat over at Nichol End. That's a pretty place. He keeps himself to himself, so you might not see him. He used to have his boat moored at Windermere until it got so busy with the tourists. Well, that's what I've heard say. He's quite an old man, so a young fellow like you might not like to be friendly. A bit of character, I understand. He's got a parrot in a cage."

Freddie listened politely as he sipped the last of his tea

and finished the final mouthfuls of his toast. Why did everyone assume that all artistic people - painters, writers, poets - wanted to be friends with each other just because they had flights of imagination in common? Not even the mention of a pet parrot roused Freddie's fancy.

"I probably won't stop in the marina for much longer than to make a quick sketch. I want to get around the whole lake and be back in time for dinner this evening. But I'll look out for the houseboat." And with those comments, he said his farewells for the day and returned to his room to seek his satchel, sketch book and pencils.

****

Edward Louis Pinner had risen early that May morning and strolled into the village at Portinscale to buy fresh bread from the bakers. He left the door and the windows of his home open and unlocked. It was safe at Derwent Water; no need to be worried about security here. When he returned, he found that the postman had already passed the marina and had left his post on the benching around *La Speranza's* prow. Edward climbed into the boat, not as nimbly or as speedily as he used to when he had first purchased her and come to live in the Lake District, but still with the skill of a man accustomed to a task. The day's delivery contained a brown manilla package bearing the stamp of the seed merchants in Liverpool that Edward favoured for seed-treats for his parrot, Guy. There was a postcard of Bath Abbey from his old friend Laurence Housman and a long white envelope bearing a London postmark. Edward neglected the seeds and postcard and immediately tore open the white envelope. Inside was a letter from his agent, based in

Bloomsbury, conveying the news that the publisher, who had in the past printed so much of his work, only found himself in a position to publish the novella Edward had recently submitted and not the longer novel.

"It's the short one, not the long one," Edward called towards the open door of the houseboat. It would mean less money. But it could be worse. The publisher could have rejected both stories, which would have meant no money.

"Looks like mutton rather than venison this month, Guy," he addressed the cabin again. "But that's better than only carrots and potatoes."

"Carrots!" came a squawk from the cabin. "Mutton!"

The door to the houseboat's cabin was low, and Edward had to stoop to enter. As he did so, it was almost as if he was paying homage to the glorious red bird, with gold-tipped wings and jewel cobalt highlights, who stood to attention in his ornate brass cage.

"Carrots! Mutton!" the parrot squawked again, staring at his owner with his bright, black, beady eyes.

"Hungry are you, you old so-and-so?" Edward asked affectionately.

He tore open the package of seeds and, taking out one of the smaller packs within, carefully poured some of the contents into a small wooden bowl which he then placed inside the cage, removing the empty dish. He pocketed the remainder of the packet, having carefully folded over the opening so that the seeds would not fall out into the insides of his trousers. Guy jumped down from his perch to the base of the cage and started to eat his seed breakfast.

"I don't suppose you're going to say thank you, are you?" Edward teased the bird.

"Mutton! Carrots!" the bird replied knowingly.

"I thought as much," Edward chuckled.

Once he had seen to Guy's breakfast, Edward made his own. With a pot of tea in front of him and two slices of fresh bread and butter with a generous spreading of last season's blackberry jam made by Mrs Porter from the village, he thought about what he would do with the day ahead. The news from his agent in London was not as good as he had hoped. He was reluctant to give up on his latest novel at the first hurdle. He had spent many months writing it, redrafting it, correcting it. He wanted it to succeed. He needed it to succeed. What else, after all, did he have to live on other than lines on a page? He would write to the agent and ask him to try a different publisher or at least be kind enough to tell him how he could improve the manuscript. Edward had worried lately that he was getting old and that living far from London in Cumbria, he was becoming out of touch. If he needed to make changes to the draft to make it more acceptable to today's modern 1930s readers, then he would do so. He just needed to be told. After all, he was an experienced writer. Under the name E.L. Pinter he had published fourteen novels, two collections of short stories and five plays, and goodness only knew how many magazine articles (the early days had been rather heady, and he couldn't remember everything from his youth with complete accuracy anymore).

Thinking of his youth reminded Edward of the postcard

from Laurence, discarded on the deck owing to the arrival of the more materially important letter from the agent. He rose to retrieve it. Laurence Housman was a good friend. A writer like himself but more successful than he had been. He hadn't seen Laurence for such a long time, not since Laurence had spent a season in the Lake District with his sister ten years ago. They had been close friends as young men, sharing the same artistic circle in London. But age had made each slower and taken one to Cumbria and the other to Somerset, counties that could hardly be farther apart.

"Laurence sends his regards from Bath," Edward told Guy. "He's bought a yellow car and engaged a driver so he can visit all his favourite places in the South. He's threatening to have the man drive him all the way up here to see us. I'd like to see that!"

It was true. It really was. He would love to see his old friend again. His heart felt heavy and lonely as he put the postcard down on the table.

"Anyway, he writes, 'Give my regards to Guy', so there you are, you old silly, you have Laurence Housman's regards."

The parrot eyed Edward seriously and chose to say nothing.

Laurence arriving in a bright yellow motor car would undoubtedly cause a stir in sleepy Portinscale, perhaps less so in the town Keswick, which was, sadly, beginning to see an increase in summer holiday tourists. It was apt that the car was yellow. Laurence always brought the sunshine with him. The summer that he and Alistair had holidayed in

Shropshire at the family home of their friend Sandro had been dingy and grey right up until the moment that Laurence had come to join them. As soon as Laurence had arrived, the sun had revealed itself to the world and beaten down on the young men intent on enjoying themselves, as if it was in a Mediterranean sky and not a British one. They had quickly abandoned the notion of sleeping inside the house and instead camped under the stars of the balmy August nights. Sandro had decided that Shropshire was indeed Greece and insisted that they all dress as Greek gods. Each one abandoned his shirt, trousers, and underwear, instead revelling in white cotton togas torn from Sandro's mother's sheets in her absence. When Clemence, Laurence's sister, had arrived for her vacation a little later, she had been horrified at the general state of nakedness among the gods on Shropshire's Mount Olympus. Despite being Laurence's sister, she was a Victorian through and through and was alarmed at any sight of flesh.

"We are artists, Clem," Sandro had slurred, sipping wine from a jug, his arm draped around Laurence's waist. "Look at Alistair's painting of Edward. Go on, Alistair, go and fetch your painting," the tipsy god demanded.

Toga-clad Alistair brought the painting out to show Clemence. On the canvas, Edward lay on the lush grass, his naked flesh absorbing and reflecting the loveliness of the August day on which it had been painted. The toga sheet, not white but grey, lilac, cream, pink, yellow, was draped across his waist and fell as a pool on the floor, obscuring all his private regions except for the shadow of curly, dark hair which crept temptingly from beneath the toga sheet towards his navel.

"I wonder what happened to that painting?" Edward asked out loud. Not to the parrot but to the air.

He reached for his pencil and notepad and jotted down 'happy summer of discovery; lost portrait of youth'. Perhaps, if he tried hard enough, he could make a new story out of that.

A little later in the morning, Freddie Booth took the path from Portinscale down towards the Nichol End marina. It was indeed a pretty place, as Mr Maddison had told him. White-painted villas and neatly kept gardens somehow seemed to have been placed there by an artist. They composed the foreground of a superb view across the crystal blue lake back to Keswick. He would return here another day to sketch and maybe come back on another to paint what he saw in watercolour. But for now, Freddie wanted to take a closer look at the boats moored at the marina he had spied from the bench on the first morning of his stay.

It was a small marina, just as small up close as it was from afar. A man was in a yacht, busily making ready for his departure now that the wind had picked up. He scarcely noticed Freddie and cast off without a nod or a smile in the young man's direction. In the corner of the marina, another man was tying up lengths of rope. He, at least, nodded a 'good morning'.

Moored up close to the wooden decking boards, Freddie recognised the houseboat, whose long, flat shape he had seen from the shore of Keswick. It was a splendid boat. *La Speranza*, he read, painted on her side. She had a dark brown hull, and a long white and grey wooden cabin with external beams and frames painted bright white. Golden-amber curtains were pulled back and tied at each window; neat and sunny now to greet the day and no doubt glowing and cosy at night.

Freddie could see a bed inside the cabin and, further along, a table, a gramophone and an empty birdcage. It was undoubtedly the home of Mr Maddison's writer, yet there was no sign of him or the bird. Freddie wasn't sure whether he felt disappointed or relieved about that. He still wanted a sketch of the boat close up, so he dropped down onto the wooden boards and pulled his sketchbook and pencil from his satchel. As before, he stabbed quickly at the paper producing vigorous lines. Once the long shape of the houseboat appeared on the virgin white paper before him, he settled into a more rhythmic motion of shading, giving the boat depth and substance.

He was so absorbed in his work that he did not notice Edward, with Guy perched on his shoulder, approach from a hut at the far end of the marina. It was more of a walk-in-cupboard than a hut, used by the owners of the boats moored at Nichol End to keep supplies of little value but great necessity. Edward had let Guy out of the cage after his breakfast, and, as usual, the parrot had accompanied him on his morning chores, with more than a little hope of some tasty titbits and bird gossip along the way. As there was no light in the hut, Edward's eyes had to work hard in the dimness to find what he had been looking for so that when he returned to the day outside, he was momentarily stunned by its brightness. He screwed up his eyes and then opened them. Before him, where there had been no one only a few moments ago, a young man with floppy sandy hair was sitting, almost sprawled on the boards, sketching his home, his houseboat. The shape of the man was familiar. The man's movements were those he had seen many times before.

"Alistair?" Edward asked, bemused, disorientated, his heart beating quickly. "Alistair, is that you?"

Freddie looked up at the old man approaching him. A man with a hopeful quizzical look and a haughty red and gold parrot on his right shoulder.

"Good morning, Sir," Freddie greeted politely.

It wasn't Alistair. Of course, it wasn't. It couldn't be.

"Oh, excuse me," Edward said, blushing. "I thought you were somebody else. I'm sorry."

Now that he was up close to the young man, Edward could see that although there was a resemblance between this lad and Alastair, he was not the same type. For a second time that morning, he was stung with loneliness.

"I hope you don't mind me sketching your boat," Freddie said, wondering from the man's expression if he had inadvertently offended with his sketchbook and pencil.

"No, not at all," Edward replied, moving closer to Freddie to see the sketch. "It's very good," he commented.

It wasn't. Not a patch on what Alistair could have done. But to say otherwise would have been rude.

"Thank you," Freddie said, unaware of the white lie.

"Potatoes!" the parrot squawked.

"Don't be so rude, you silly old thing," Edward chided his bird.

Freddie's face was a picture of astonishment.

"Did that bird just speak?" he asked incredulously. "Did it say 'potatoes'?"

"He certainly did, the rude fellow," Edward chuckled. "He seems to be a bird of moderate intelligence and has learned the words of a few vegetables and suchlike. 'Potatoes', I'm afraid, is not a compliment. Now that he has been rude to you, I think it just as well that he is introduced."

Freddie hastened to his feet, unsure what would happen next.

"I am Edward Pinner, otherwise known as the writer E.L Pinter and this is Guy, my parrot."

"Freddie Booth."

Edward extended a hand to Freddie's to be met with a shake, and Guy held out a claw.

"Do I shake it?" Freddie asked wide-eyed.

"If you want him to like you, I suggest you do."

Gingerly, Freddie reached for the parrot's claw with his finger and thumb to take it in a quick shake.

Edward chuckled again at the young man's reticence.

"To seal the friendship, you had better give him something to eat."

Edward reached into his pocket for the remainder of the seed packet he had given the bird at breakfast and indicated that he wanted to pour it onto Freddie's open hand. The young man raised his palm, now a cup of seeds, to the parrot's beak. Guy pecked gently at the soft flesh, eagerly sucking the tasty seed treats into his throat.

"Carrots! Carrots!" the parrot pronounced enthusiastically.

"Ah, he likes you," Edward said. "Now, young man, would you like to come on board and see the boat you've drawn and have a cup of coffee?"

Freddie did not immediately respond to the invitation. He had planned to spend the day alone walking around the lake, stopping only to sketch. But now, he was presented with the opportunity of seeing inside the beautiful houseboat that had attracted his attention so much that he had drawn it twice, once from afar in Keswick and once up close from the marina's edge. Yet the visit would cause a delay to his self-imposed schedule, and it would imply acceptance of a friendship offered. A friendship that he was not sure he could be bothered to accept.

"Or perhaps you have other things to do this morning and don't have the time?" Edward said, offering Freddie a reason to decline his invitation.

There was something in the old writer's voice that seemed so sad when he said this that Freddie felt guilty.

"Thank you, yes, I will. It's very kind, Mr Pinner," he replied, justifying to himself that the houseboat was charming and that he'd never been aboard such a vessel before.

"Call me Edward, please," Edward said with a smile almost of relief.

"Thank you, Edward."

Freddie climbed into the *La Speranza*, following his host.

Despite fleeing to the Lake District this Spring, when Valerie Pearson had rejected his proposal, Freddie was not experienced in boats. He had learned to row as a boy but had never sailed. His family, wealthy enough, were not the sort to take cruises abroad nor purchase yachts as symbols of status. The attraction of the Lake District was that it was far from London and that his family would pay for his board and lodging and leave him alone to sketch, paint and forget. Usually, when Freddie observed boats, he felt he would have to do something if he boarded. He would be obliged to pick up oars and exert energy to make the vessel pass through the water. He would need to understand the technicalities of ropes and winds to persuade a yacht to move any distance. Edward's houseboat was entirely different. It had a motor that required no effort other than turning it on. It had a wheel to steer it, which could be no different from the motorcar he drove at home. And, very importantly, there was a cabin to keep him safe and dry if the weather should become hostile to a fair-weather boatman such as himself. As a result, he felt relaxed and almost at home.

He stooped to enter the cabin, which was neat and surprisingly airy. He made to sit down on a free-standing chair.

"Not there," Edward stopped him. "That's my writing chair," he smiled apologetically. "Take a seat at the bench."

"Of course, I'm sorry," Freddie said, not wanting to offend any more than he felt he had already done that morning.

He took the space at the bench that Edward indicated, his back to the window and facing into the cabin, finding it gave him more opportunity to look at the objects in his new acquaintance's life than his first choice of chair would have done. The section of the cabin where he sat was Edward's living and working area. There was little on view to show that he was a writer besides a notepad, a pencil on the table, and a shelf of books. Wedged between the books was a photograph of a man, a relative perhaps, in a gleaming silver frame. Further along, was the sleeping area. Two beds, neatly made with patchwork coverlets, were twins to each other on either side of the cabin. Evidently, Edward's was made ready for the night to come, and the other was strewn with cushions so that it was more of a sofa than a bed.

The whole boat, like Edward, was neat, tidy, and clean. It made Freddie feel grubby and unkempt, even though he knew deep down that he wasn't. Unconsciously, he ran his fingers through his floppy straw hair to neaten his appearance and be a more presentable guest.

Edward looked at the young man out of the corner of his eye as he bustled around his houseboat home - putting Guy back into his cage with a drink of water, preparing the coffee, serving the last pieces of Mrs Buntings' shortbread onto a plate - regretting that he was going to share it but also pleased that he had a guest to share it with. He saw the young man study his home carefully, probably also studying him. For a moment, he shivered. Edward Pinner did not like to be studied. Yet he had invited the young man onto the boat, into his home, so did his guest not have a right to be curious?

Yes, it was curiosity he saw in Freddie's face, not judgement.

Edward placed the two cups of hot coffee on the table in front of his guest.

"You're an artist?" he enquired, stating the obvious.

"Not really," Freddie replied awkwardly.

"But you were sketching my boat. Perhaps it is more of a hobby?"

"Not really," Freddie said again, adding a sigh.

Freddie saw that his host was confused by his responses. He was confused himself.

"I suppose you could say that I enjoy drawing and painting, and I *intend* to make it pay - does that make me an artist?"

As he spoke, he looked at Edward with the fierce intensity of a child who had done poorly and who promised this time to do better. Although twenty-two years old, there was much of the child still in his face, in the softness in the cheeks, the paucity of lines around the eyes. But at the same time, there was the maturing man's chiselled bone structure and the fine furrows of experience and wisdom which were gently beginning to indent themselves onto his brow.

Freddie's was a pleasant face, a kind face, Edward thought. A face which reminded him of Alistair. His eyes flicked to the photograph on the shelf. Alistair, too had had the money from his parents to be able to intend to succeed in the world of art, and he had - as much as he had wanted to.

"May I see your sketch book?" Edward asked.

Freddie's hand immediately flew to the satchel on the bench. It was a defensive move. A gesture to protect what lay within. Inside his sketchbook were his thoughts on paper. For the past few weeks, he had sketched every day, rarely looking back at the preceding page to evaluate, analyse or improve. Each day he had drawn with speed, as a mad man. He knew that although he had, on occasion, been pleased with his efforts, he certainly wasn't proud of the work that the book contained.

"I won't be offended if you don't want to," Edward said, reading Freddie's expression correctly. "Only another artist would understand the great privacy of a sketchbook or a notebook."

Freddie smiled with relief, bringing the boy back into the room.

"Another time, perhaps?" he offered.

"That would be a privilege and something to look forward to."

Which meant, of course, as they both now knew, that Freddie would come back.

Freddie did not make it any further around the lake that day. When he had drunk his coffee and eaten his shortbread, he found that the conversation had taken them into the world of Edward's books, the stories he had written, the difficulties in bringing the ideas in his head to paper, to book, to publication. The literary world that Edward revealed to him was not a world Freddie knew. It fascinated him, and he stayed in the houseboat long into the afternoon.

"Did you meet the writer?" Mr Maddison asked Freddie at breakfast the following day.

"Yes, I did as it happens."

"Strange old fellow, is he? That's what I've heard."

"No stranger than you or I!" Freddie laughed.

"Well, it takes a certain sort to live on a boat like that, but he's probably harmless enough," was Mr Maddison's verdict, thinking to himself that perhaps artists were allowed to be different.

"And did you see the parrot?" he continued.

"Yes, I did. It talks."

"Well, I never! What did it say?"

"Potatoes."

****

May merged into June, and Freddie found his feet taking him on the path that led away from Keswick and around to the Nichol End marina most days. To reach it, he had to head north out of the town, away from the lake. Then, almost at the edge of the town, he turned sharp left taking the path adjacent to the old stone bridge crossing the river Greta. The route now traversed fields, and it seemed to be taking him further away from, not closer to, the lake waters. On either side, the hills rose to lavender peaks on the horizon, guarding and cradling the lake. At length, the path connected with the main road to Cockermouth and led him to a second bridge with stone arches gracefully spanning the river Derwent, which fed the lake from the North. The road now took him up into Portinscale. Hardly a breath from the village, he found the woodland track leading to the lake and the Nicole End Marina.

On one such day, Edward was looking out for him on the boat's prow.

"I thought we might take *La Speranza* out on the lake this morning. She's been moored up here too long. It will do her good, and me too. Would you like that?" he called as he saw Freddie approaching.

Freddie's broad smile was all Edward needed to know as a response.

It was just as Freddie had thought. Manoeuvring the houseboat through the lake water was as close to driving a motor car as he could have imagined. He felt a thrill as the boat cut through the water, accompanied by the low rumble of the engine, and saw the landscape pass quickly by. As there was no wind that morning, they were alone on the lake, apart from a handful of pleasure rowers. Edward steered the boat close to the western shore so that Freddie could see all the pretty bays and coves which lay along it.

"You'd be able to paint some good pictures from this direction, don't you think?" Edward commented, enjoying the view thoroughly himself.

"Perhaps."

"Maybe you should try?"

"Later, maybe."

"You are a good artist, you know," Edward encouraged. "And you are getting better all the time. It takes practice as well as talent."

Freddie was silent. He gazed at the lake's edge, the shingle and boulders of the bay they were passing, and the couple of trees which seemed to be falling off it into the water, held back only by an intricate lacing of roots. What would hold onto him if he allowed himself to fall? he wondered.

"I didn't come to the Lakes this summer to paint, you know," he confessed to Edward.

"You didn't?" Edward replied. He had thought as much.

"No, I came here to forget."

Edward waited for Freddie to tell him what he wanted to forget.

"Have you ever been married?" Freddie asked Edward innocently, almost seeming to change the subject of the conversation.

"No," Edward replied. He wished that he had.

Freddie was too caught up in his own thoughts to hear the note of regret in his friend's voice.

"I wanted to get married, you know."

"Oh really?"

"Yes. To a girl called Valerie Pearson. We met at a party in London last Christmas. She was very pretty and laughed a lot."

"And what happened?"

"She didn't like me as much as I liked her." It still hurt him to think it, even more, to say it.

Edward nodded in consolation. Being pretty and laughing a lot was not the foundation for a life-long relationship, but the young man needed to find that out for himself.

"So she said no, and you came here for your art."

"Yes," Freddie said ruefully, thinking now as he stood on the deck of the houseboat beside this man who lived on the lake for his art and earned his living from his art that just maybe he had been a little ridiculous and overly romantic.

"Sometimes, we all need to run away for a while," Edward said quietly. "And some of our best work can be produced when we do. You do have talent Freddie," he continued. "You just need more…"

"Practice!" Freddie completed with a smile.

"Exactly!" Edward said with enough enthusiasm for them both. "Let's go back to Nicole End. I'll write this morning, and you can sketch."

And seizing the moment, instead of hugging the eastern length of the shore to show his young friend those views, he steered his boat back north through the centre of the lake, taking it to its maximum speed as he did so. The two men laughed as *La Speranza* cut through the water and their faces cut through the air, and the sombreness of regret that had hung over them both only a few moments ago was left behind.

****

June blossomed into double digits, and as it did, some welcome news arrived for Edward; another postcard from Laurence, this time of Worcester cathedral, announcing that he fully did intend to have his chauffeur drive him north and imminently.

"Another postcard from Laurence," Edward told Guy, holding up the postcard to the cage for the bird to see as if the bird cared. "No 'regards' this time for you, though. Perhaps he'll give them to you himself when he comes."

It was with something akin to nervousness that Edward headed into Keswick a week later. He tended not to go into the town much, preferring to stay in little Portinscale. He had told Freddie that he would be busy today but did not give a reason. He noticed the surprise in Freddie's eyes. It hadn't occurred to him that Edward could have anything to do besides be on or around his boat writing. Edward hurried the short way over the bridges and across the fields, hoping that he would not run into Freddie as he did so. He felt a need for secrecy. He didn't want to share his old friend with his new one - yet.

Edward entered the lounge at the Keswick hotel next to the station, built in the last century when the railway had arrived, and stood on the threshold looking around the room. A man wearing a three-piece cream suit and with an expertly trimmed pointed grey beard and dapper moustache was sitting, legs crossed, in an armchair reading a newspaper.

"Laurence!" Edward called out across the room despite himself. He ought to have approached the reader quietly and have gently announced his presence with an attention-seeking cough or a low 'good afternoon', but the sight of his old friend sitting in such a familiar pose, after so many years, was too much for Edward and he threw habitual caution the wind.

Laurence Housman looked up, and his face broke into the brightest of smiles.

"Edward, my dear chap," he exclaimed warmly, rising to embrace his friend. "How are you? You look well enough! And how's that old bird of yours?"

"We're both well. Oh, Laurence, it is so good to see you." Edward could feel the faint pricks of tears at his eyelashes. It was funny how happiness can be so painful, he thought briefly, as Laurence invited him to sit in an adjacent armchair and caught the waitress's eye to order a cup of tea for them both.

"How is Clemence?" Edward asked.

"She's well, thank you. She didn't want to come cavorting in the car with me. She's slowed down a lot recently."

"We all have, haven't we?" Edward commented, feeling his age.

"Not me, not a bit. Plenty of go left in me!" Laurence smiled.

"How long will you stay?"

"Not long. Just a few days. I'm due in London next week."

"London? I thought you and Clemence left that behind years ago?"

"She did, but I couldn't keep away. I've taken a bachelor pad. It's useful for going to the rehearsals for my plays too."

"Plays?"

Edward was dimly aware that he had missed chapters of his friend's life, hidden away in the Lake District as he was.

"Oh yes, plenty of plays. I'll tell you about them," Laurence said. If he had noticed that Edward had not known about his plays, he didn't show it. If he was upset by Edward's ignorance, he hid it. Laurence lived in the moment, rarely harbouring judgements or regrets, and he enjoyed holding forth to an audience. The rest of the afternoon would be very pleasant, regaling Edward with the plots of his plays and their increasing success whilst sipping tea in the lounge of the Keswick hotel.

It rained the next day - heavy and hard. Laurence had his chauffeur Wilfred Wills drive him over to Portinscale in the middle of the morning with instructions to collect him at the end of the afternoon. Wills was used to such a direction. He had a comfortable relationship with his employer whereby as long as he was ready and able to take Housman wherever he wanted, whenever he wanted, the rest of the time was his - as well as the use of the car. It was a shame today was so wet. Wills would have liked to have driven around Derwent Water and across to Windermere, but there was little point if he could hardly see out past the windscreen wipers. He would return to the hotel and the papers.

Laurence strolled down to the boat under a black umbrella.

"*La Speranza* - Hope," he said admiringly before boarding the boat and seeking the protection of the cabin.

"Guy! My dear friend!" he exclaimed, bowing to the parrot in the cage, as all who entered the cabin were forced to do.

"Mutton! Carrots!!" Guy squawked.

"It's good to see you too, you silly old bird," Laurence replied. "But my, he's showing his age now, Edward. He's not quite as sleek and bright as he once was, is he?"

"Well, we're all getting on a bit, aren't we? It's not the 1890s anymore," Edward replied, opening the cage. He hadn't noticed that Guy looked like an old bird. Maybe Laurence saw things differently.

Guy was just as pleased with the visit of an old friend as Edward was. He hopped enthusiastically onto Laurence's outstretched arm, travelled up to his shoulder where he sat, and nuzzled his ear.

The two friends passed a very happy time together, lunching on the boat. Having spoken at length of his own literary projects the day before, Laurence quizzed Edward on his today. They talked about the rejected novel. Edward welcomed Laurence's observations and suggestions. For a few hours, it was almost as if they were their former selves again, creating, discussing, and arguing in salons full of cigarette smoke. He did not, however, tell Laurence about Freddie. It wasn't that he needed to keep Freddie to himself. No, he had always socialised with Laurence when others had been around. It was more that he wasn't sure just what Laurence would make of Freddie. Yet carefully avoiding mentioning Freddie brought the realisation that he hadn't seen the lad for two days now and was missing him.

"The weather is likely to be better tomorrow," Laurence said before leaving. "Do you fancy a spin in the Daimler? We could go down to Windermere if you like or to one of the other lakes. Let's take a picnic. I'll order one from the hotel."

"Thank you. I'd like to very much," Edward replied brightly. "But may I bring a friend? He's a young artist. I'm sure he'd like to join us."

"Of course. That would be delightful. Is he…?" He didn't finish his question, merely raised an enquiring eyebrow.

"No," Edward replied.

"Ah well, never mind, we will all have a nice day anyway."

It was, as it happened, a lovely day. The sun had returned to a blue sky, and the day had remembered that it was summer and that it was allowed to be warm. Edward had sent Freddie a note via the errand boy at the bakery, who, for a few pennies, had bicycled over to the Belle Vue boarding house. They now stood waiting in Portinscale on the road alongside a garden of pink roses ornamenting a white-painted villa to be collected by Laurence and his motor car.

The bright yellow Daimler arrived soon after, its paintwork gleaming in the sunshine. It was beautiful - elegant and bright like Laurence. Edward was right, the car did cause a stir. Some little boys playing in a front garden could not resist creeping out from beyond the gate to view the butter-bright vehicle, even though such an action risked reprimand from parents indoors. Mrs Bunting, who kept Edward supplied with delicious shortbread, saw the party on her way to the baker's and called,

"Out for the day then, Mr Pinner?"

"Yes, Mrs Bunting," he answered. "My friend is taking us for a spin in his motor, and we will stop for a picnic."

She was quite taken with the boyish enthusiasm for the outing that was written all over his face.

"Well, I'm sure you will have a lovely day," She nodded a good-morning acknowledgement to Laurence, Freddie, and Wills, the driver, before proceeding to the bakers. What a nice change it was for poor Mr Pinner to have some friends visit. She knew he was lonely. She silently said a prayer for their day to be full of blessings. And it was.

Wills drove them first to Thirlmere, then to Grasmere, through Ambleside - almost a twin to Keswick, and on to Windermere. Around Windemere, the landscape became more open and more rolling. The lavender peaks of the northern Lakes were replaced by green hills - gentler but just as lovely. They stopped for their picnic lunch on the shores of the lake, just past the southern tip. Here, Laurence, Edward and Freddie took a stroll while Wills stayed with the car. Freddie picked up a thumb-sized flat stone and, standing side-on to the water, twisted his body, throwing the stone under his arm to make it bounce on the water's surface, not once, not twice, but three times, before it sank, leaving only a trail of ripples. Laurence, not to be outdone, picked up a similar size stone and matched the three bounces before his stone sank. Edward sat down to watch the good-natured skimming competition that ensued, not worrying that the day's schedule had been interrupted by play. On the way home, they broke the journey for afternoon tea at Grasmere, making Darjeeling toasts to Wordsworth, who had lived there 130 years before, and eating scones overburdened with strawberry jam and thick cream. All the way along, they joked and chatted, discussed, and admired, and even sometimes sat in silence, enjoying each other's company and the stunning landscape.

Laurence had only one more day of his visit left. He could not persuade Edward to dine with him in Keswick but readily accepted the invitation to eat on the houseboat along with Guy. It was more basic, but it was comfortable. The boat was a place where they could let their guard down - a place where they were not on show. On the evening before Laurence's departure, they stood together, side by side in the empty marina, looking out across the water towards Keswick. Small figures near small boats were barely distinguishable to their seventy-year-old eyes.

"Do you like Freddie?" Edward asked candidly.

"He's quite green, isn't he," Laurence commented in response.

"He can't help his age," Edward replied defensively, feeling that Laurence ought to have said something kinder.

"I know, I know," Laurence admitted. "As it happens, I have a young friend too."

"Do you really?" Edward was surprised. Laurence had not mentioned anyone special in his infrequent letters and postcards, nor at any time during the last few days.

"Yes, Reggie Reynolds, he's a Quaker and an intellectual."

"Is he...?" Edward paused. "Is he like us?"

"Goodness gracious no!" Laurence laughed. "That would be far too complicated."

"But does he know?"

"Yes. I'm very open with Reggie. We both discuss our love affairs as well as our artistic ones."

"And how did he take it when you told him?"

"I didn't need to. He worked it out for himself."

Edward sat for a moment in silence. He was sure that Freddie had no idea how he and Laurence, Alistair, Sandro and others like them had lived and loved in secret. What would his reaction be if he knew? Would he adopt an enlightened, accepting view, as Laurence's friend Reggie had, or would he take the law's perspective and be unforgiving?

"I can see that your young friend, Freddie, doesn't know," Laurence said gravely. "Are you going to let him continue in his innocence? Or are you going to show him who you really are?"

Edward's eyes grew wide in panic at the scene Laurence was writing for his life.

"It's … It's not safe." Edward stuttered. "I couldn't tell him. Better for him to think of me as he does - as a bit of a mad old uncle. I don't want to lose him."

Laurence nodded in sympathy and understanding.

"What I'd like to know, Edward, my old friend," Laurence said, his ordinarily merry eyes now still and solemn. "Is why you allowed this young man to become close to you?"

Why? Why had he? He couldn't explain it. A passing resemblance to Alistair? A yearning for youth? Genuinely hitting it off as friends despite the decades between each other?

"Maybe Reggie and Freddie are the sons we could never have," Edward said at length.

"Or the grandsons."

There was a hint of regret in Laurence Housman's voice too.

****

Laurence's visit ended. The summer solstice came and went. On most days, Freddie and Edward worked side by side on Edward's boat. Freddie had begun to rework his early summer sketches, either tidying them up or starting them afresh, learning from his mistakes. Inspired by Laurence Housman's success with the theatre, Edward abandoned his unsuccessful novel and started writing a play about James I, King of England. The days were comfortable, rain or shine.

Freddie would have breakfast at the Belle Vue boarding house and take lunch and afternoon tea with Edward. He would return to Keswick to dine at his lodgings on a substantial meal prepared by Mrs French, the cook. As the days passed, he found his trousers were tighter around the middle than at the beginning of the summer and chided himself for too much sitting around and too much good food. The daily walk to Nicole End and back was evidently not enough to balance the hearty meals he was consuming, so he began taking an additional evening walk around the town or along the lake to the south.

It had been a particularly hot day in the middle of July. Edward and Freddie had given up working on the houseboat, which was in full sun and had turned hour by hour into an oven attempting to roast them alive. Instead, they had sought the cool shade of the trees by the next bay, where they had sat smoking cigarettes, their backs up against the rough bark enjoying each other's company and the soporific lapping of the water on the stones. Freddie went back to his lodgings, as usual, in the early evening to eat his meal and take his walk, letting the sound of the rippling water and smell of the moist air speak to his senses. When he returned at length to the Belle Vue, the long day was still bright even though it was well past closing time at the Four in Hand pub next door. Not feeling in the least bit sleepy, Freddie was not inclined to go to bed. Not when there still seemed so much more of the day left to be lived, especially now that it was finally cool enough to live it. He turned his back on the pub and the Belle Vue and marched resolutely down the hill towards the shores of the Derwent Water.

There was no one about. The still water was a sheet of grey steel stretched over the unknown depths of the lake. Freddie glanced over to the marina where Edward's boat was moored. Edward had drawn the curtains for the night, and light from within illuminated the fabric, turning each pane to a bright amber eye staring at Freddie across the water.

With no regard for the lateness of the evening, Freddie turned his feet in the direction of his friend's houseboat home. The night was darker when he arrived at the marina than it had been when he had left the pub; for an instant, he remembered it was late. Summer nights make Time a liar. He glanced at his watch - 11.20 pm. Was it too late for a visit? For a heartbeat, he regretted his venture.

The golden cloth of the curtains had been stretched tightly across each window in all but one place. For some reason, and Freddie would never be able to explain why exactly, he hesitated from boarding the boat and greeting his friend. Instead, he crept up to the edge of the *La Speranza* and leaned his face against the glass, where a sliver of the boat's interior was revealed to him by the lone gap in the curtains.

Inside there was a woman. She was sitting on Edward's writing chair with her back to the window. Guy was preening himself on his stand. There was no sign of Edward.

Who could the woman be? Freddie felt irritated. Edward had not mentioned that a female friend would visit him, but neither had he said anything in advance about Laurence Housman's arrival. He looked closely at all he could see of her, wanting to recognise her as a Cumbrian local and not a female interloper from Edward's other life. The woman's deep chestnut hair was cut in a flapper bob, the style of several years earlier. Puffs of smoke emanated from her cigarette and disappeared into the cabin. She sat with her legs crossed, and from his position at the window, Freddie could see that her legs were shapely in black silk stockings. Beading from the fringe of her dress, rustled almost imperceptibly at her knees, as the reeds at the far end of Derwent Water hardly dared to whisper when the air was still.

The parrot looked straight at the woman, and the woman said something to the parrot which Freddie could not hear. The fact that Guy was comfortable in this strange woman's presence bothered Freddie. He was pierced with jealousy that Edward had a female friend whom the parrot tolerated, perhaps even liked.

The woman stood up. Instinctively Freddie stepped back from where he had been peeping in at the window, withdrawing into the shadows so as not to be seen. His heart quickened. Glancing around, he checked that the marina was as deserted as it had been when he had arrived. The thick shadows hid no one but himself. There was still no sign of Edward, on or off the boat.

Freddie moved back to the window and again pressed his eye to the glass between the accidental gap in the curtains. Inside the cabin, the woman had put a shining black disk onto the gramophone, and Freddie could hear the music's muffled melody. She had stubbed out her cigarette on the dish on the table. Guy, the parrot, watched the woman from his stand and Freddie, the voyeur, watched her from the glass beyond as she slowly moved her hips to the rhythm of the music. She danced sensuously, performing to the parrot, all the time with her back to Freddie at the window. The gramophone's needle reached the end of the grooves in the disk. With no more furrows of music, it spun round and around, uttering a hiss of non-sound where a few seconds before, there had been melody. The woman ignored it. Instead, she reached round to the nape of her neck and undid the button. She then lifted the silver satin dress over her shoulders, the beading momentarily becoming entangled with her chestnut hair, and dropped it on the cabin floor in front of the parrot as if a gift.

She now stood before the parrot in her underwear - a lace-trimmed corset cum brassiere. The skin around her lower arms, free from the dress, hung with loose flesh that in earlier years had been filled. Then placing her left hand on her hip and her right behind her head, the woman posed for the parrot's appreciation before bending over and removing her black silk stockings.

Freddie stood on the marina's side, his eye glued to the crack of light coming from the houseboat window. He could not have moved even if a policeman had come along and asked him his business. Who was this woman? Why in heaven's name was she taking her clothes off so seductively, performing to a parrot, and where the hell was Edward? Watching her dance stirred him. It stirred his groin.

The woman was enjoying herself. She stroked her black silk stockings tenderly but also with an appreciation of their quality, as if sipping expensive wine before she placed them on the houseboat floor in front of the parrot's cage. With a deft move that must have taken years of practice, she removed her underwear. Now she stood naked, her buttocks to the window, her breasts to the parrot. Only then did she move to the gramophone and refresh the disk. Only then did she turn round in full frontal nakedness to face Freddie at the window. Her eyes looked up and out into the dark, where she saw Freddie in the gap the curtain had not filled. Her eyes locked with Freddie's, and her face reflected Freddie's horror.

Freddie turned tail and ran, retreating into the shadows. He fled like a thief who had stolen a precious jewel, heading for the lakeside field, where he vomited into a bramble bush.

"Freddie!" Edward, now wrapped in a velvet bathrobe, called shakily from the deck of the houseboat.

"Freddie!" he whispered, the glossy hairs of his wig catching the sparkle of the moonlight.

****

Perhaps it wasn't Freddie's choice that he stopped visiting Edward. The Lake District was not so many miles from London, and first, Freddie's younger brother Henry, newly graduated from Oxford, arrived for a short vacation. He stayed with Freddie at the Belle Vue boarding house and, taking inspiration from the name, persuaded Freddie to seek out those famous local views. They started with the Catbells path, high above Derwent Water; they explored Skiddaw, and once Freddie's fitness had caught up with his younger brother's, they tackled Scafell Pike. In those heights, Freddie discovered a rough and ready landscape that he found aggressive and manly. Returning to the Belle Vue, he picked up his oil paints and, with Mr Maddison's permission, made a studio for himself in an outhouse at the rear where he daubed canvases with slices and stabs of sticky colour.

No sooner had Henry departed than his cousin Amelia came to stay, bringing her friend Dorothy with her as a companion. They admired his oils of the peaks but preferred his watercolours of the lake. They were water babies. They chose to spend their time in or on the lake. Freddie hired boats for them daily and, with increasing confidence, rowed them across Derwent Water or to the southern shore, never the northern. He sat comfortably back in his seat when they took the oars, a long beam apiece, giggling at their efforts. On the days that the sun was hot and the weather warm, the girls donned their swimming costumes and decorated caps and dipped their toes, then their limbs, into the cool, dark water of the lake.

Freddie had met Dorothy once before at a party in London that he had attended with Valerie. She was a pretty girl, quite bookish. She laughed at his witticism when it was funny and complimented his work when it was good. He had a vague impression of loss when she departed with Amelia towards the end of August, but he had no interest in discovering whether it was a loss he felt or a loss he saw in her eyes as they bid their farewells.

With long summer evenings on his hands that could no longer be filled in the company of Edward at his boat or by the feminine charms of Dorothy and his sister in the guests' drawing room at the Belle Vue boarding house, Freddie found the lure of the Four Hands pub next door too great a temptation to resist. He quickly fell into the habit of spending the day painting the paths of the peaks around Derwent Water, vistas embedded in his memory from the walks he had undertaken with his brother a few weeks earlier. He would pause only for a light lunch. At the end of the afternoon, he would tidy up his little studio, wash his brushes and clean his hands. A light stroll along the shoreline south of Keswick preceded his supper at the boarding house and his evenings in the pub.

The Four Hands retained its Victorian interior. It was dark and smoky inside. It was somewhere he could lose himself and forget about the betrayal - first Valerie's, then Edward's. He would never have drunk in such a building in London. At home, he drank at parties or from his parents' cocktail bar in their posh new London flat. One or two of his friends were members of clubs, and occasionally he was invited there to dine and become gently inebriated. Here it was different. Here it was possible to drink and drink in a dark hole and stagger next door home to bed.

The pub was more the domain of the locals than the tourists. They left Freddie alone in the corner, feeling more miserable than he had any time since Valerie Pearson had rejected him. The landlord was pleasant enough, although he deliberately seemed to take his time before serving Freddie each newly ordered pint.

It had been at least a month since he had watched the striptease - a month in which he had not seen Edward and had worked very hard not to think about him. He was sitting in an alcove of the pub where he could not be seen and from which he could see little. It was a hole, and it suited him. After a while, he was vaguely aware that a group of men had come in and were sitting at the table on the other side of the alcove. They may have been there for some time. He didn't know. He didn't usually listen to other people's conversations, but the phrases he could hear being used resonated with his subconscious and without trying, he found he was eavesdropping.

"It's disgusting and not natural," he heard one voice say.

"I say we teach him a lesson," a second voice added. "Just to warn him - warn him we're watching him, and we don't want none of that business up here."

"Disgusting. Filthy. Like I said."

"We can show him, and that bloody parrot too, what filthy is," a different voice said with a chill that went straight through Freddie.

Freddie tried to get up and manoeuvre himself into a position where he could see the men's faces without drawing attention.

"Tonight?" the first voice questioned.

"Nah. If we're going to do it, we have to do it right. We

need to think it through."

By the time Freddie had placed himself where he might be able to see who the speakers were, or at least any details about them that would make them distinguishable, they had stood up to leave and were already walking away. From behind, they could have been anybody.

He watched them leave the pub, the door swinging shut behind them, so he returned to his seat in the corner and his half-finished pint. He lit a cigarette and smoked it as he finished the brown liquid in his glass. It was unnatural, he thought. It was filthy. And then he felt sick as much by himself as by these thoughts, the ale, and the smoke.

****

He rehearsed what he would say to Edward with every step he took from Keswick to Nichol End the next day. He had battled with himself during the night and knew he could not leave Edward unprotected. In his mind, he decided that he would be brief. He would make it clear that he had no desire to be involved by association with such revolting behaviour. He could not say that exactly, so it would be in his manner of talking to the old man. But, he would make it equally clear that even though Edward was disgusting to anyone with morals, Freddie would not knowingly allow Edward to be hurt or his property mistreated. Despite all the hundreds of steps it took to reach the marina, when he arrived there, he still did not know for sure what he would say or how he would say it.

The marina was busier than he had seen it before. August brought tourists to each corner and bay of the lake. Freddie marched up to the houseboat.

"Mr Pinner," he called.

There was silence. No answer.

Freddie looked inside the cabin. Guy was in his cage, but Edward was not visible.

"Blast!" he said quietly.

There was nothing for it but to leave the old man a note. At least that way, Freddie thought, he would have done his duty.

He boarded the *La Speranza* and turned the cabin door handle. It was unlocked, as he knew it would be.

"Potatoes!" Guy squawked angrily when Freddie entered.

"Pleased to see you too, Guy," Freddie replied sarcastically.

"Potatoes, potatoes, potatoes," Guy repeated. It was strange how a bird could make a mere vegetable sound so vicious and threatening.

"Don't worry, Guy, I'm not going to stay. I want to leave Edward a message."

Edward's notebook was on the table. Freddie picked it up and turned hastily to a fresh page, trying hard not to look at the notes that Edward had made therein, as if the notebook were a diary filled with secrets that ought not to be shared. Yet flicking through, his eyes took in the words 'happy summer of discovery, lost portrait of youth', written in the middle of a page and encircled several times.

'Disgusting!' Freddie thought. 'How dare the old pervert write about him!'

He found a fresh page and hastily scribbled his message - to lock the cabin doors, be wary of strangers and live quietly. Reading it through, he wasn't sure it didn't look like a threat, so he added a sentence to say that he had overheard the vicious talk and signed it 'with all best wishes'.

Guy was watching him suspiciously throughout.

"You'd better look after him," Freddie said to the bird as he left the cabin, closing the door behind him.

"Carrots!" was the muffled response from behind the door.

A little later, Edward returned home and found the note.

"So, he's been here?" he said to Guy, adding a sigh. "It's a shame he couldn't stay."

Then he tore Freddie's message from the notebook. The lad must be overreacting to some local gossip.

"We're safe at Nicole End, aren't we, Guy? No one would hurt us here?" Guy did not reply. He fixed his eye on Edward before pecking at the cage door, showing that he wanted to be let out.

"Alright then, you old silly," Edward answered.

Guy, released from the cage, flew around the cabin and landed on Edward's writing chair.

"Ah, so you think I should write, do you? You're probably right." He tore up Freddie's message and put the pieces of the note into the bin. No one would hurt them. No one.

Sitting down, he pulled the notebook towards himself and flicked through. He had not been as productive this summer as he needed to be. The play about James I was going nowhere, although it had started well enough in the afterglow of Laurence's visit. He had picked and prodded at the novel that the publisher had rejected. Hacking it back, dissecting it, rewriting passages, and generally making it worse than before he had started. Laurence's visit had been a welcome tonic; during the summer, in the hours he had spent with Freddie, he had felt uplifted - young again. If he had met Freddie as a young man, he would have been instantly attracted to him. He was so like Alistair, and yet he wasn't Alistair.

He had met Alistair at a lecture on Michelangelo at the Royal Academy. Alistair was studying the form of the nude through the ages to assist his painting, and Edward was researching an idea for a short story that was never written in the end. Edward saw Alistair sitting alone in a row close enough to the front to hear and see clearly, but not so far forward to be noticed. The young man was lovely, exquisite. He had floppy sandy hair that fell over his eyes and needed to be pushed back into place every few minutes. It was both a boy's face and a man's face at the same time. The seat alongside him was empty. Edward approached.

"Excuse me, is this seat free? May I sit here?" he asked nervously.

Alistair turned and smiled. A beam of sunlight fell there and then upon Edward and stayed on him until cruelly extinguished by influenza nearly 30 years later. As Edward sat down, he let his hand accidentally brush against Alistair's thigh. There was no flinch, no pulling away, only a drawing together.

The pages of the notebook flicked before his eyes, and the book fell open where he had last made notes of any use: 'happy summer of discovery; lost portrait of youth'. Perhaps there was a story in that, he thought, as he had before. But whose story it was now - his or Freddie's - he no longer knew.

****

Mr Maddison was concerned about young Mr Booth. The lad had arrived at the beginning of May shrouded in emotional turmoil. He had been an adolescent full of anger, unpredictable in his silences and sudden bursts of energy. In the early summer, he had calmed down. He had shown himself to be reasonable and even good company. He had applied himself thoughtfully to his art and had shown Mr Maddison, and Mrs French too, some of his sketches and watercolours, which were rather good, so he had permitted Freddie to use his outhouse for oil painting. But something was wrong. The lad was taciturn and grumpy. Moreover, he was evidently spending the evenings next door at the pub, as his bedroom had the vile odour of stale alcohol in the morning when the maid went in to clean. This swing from good humour back to bad had coincided with the departure of that pretty girl, the friend of Mr Booth's sister. Mr Maddison put Freddie's melancholy anger down to another case of love sickness. Two cases in one summer were exhausting for any young man. So Mr Maddison continued to treat Freddie just as kindly as he could.

Leaving Edward a warning note had done nothing to calm Freddie's fears. He didn't worry about the man during the day. It was the night that would bring the trouble if there was to be any. Freddie deliberately looked over to the marina on his evening walks, checking from afar that all was well. Two evenings later, when he looked over at the boat, something was not well. Something was not right. Freddie couldn't tell for sure what it was - not from the other side of the lake. All he knew was that something did not feel right.

It was dark now. The fullness of night had descended. Freddie ran out of the town, grateful to the streetlamps along the way. Across the fields, there were no lights. He had to trust his memory. The moon was hidden behind clouds, rarely producing a finger of light. When he reached the marina, Freddie hurried over to the boat. The lights were off inside the cabin, and the door was ajar. The normally pristine grey and white paint of the boat was covered along the marina side and around the cabin door entrance in dark smears of what looked like paint but smelt of excrement. Freddie vaulted over the prow and leapt in through the door. The inside of the cabin was full of shadows and the bitter stench of urine. He went to turn on the light. Nothing happened. The bulbs did not bring light. The boat remained full of darkness. Delving into his pockets, Freddie took his box of matches and lit a flame. In the flickering matchlight, he could see that the inside of the cabin was in disarray. The orderly books that had been on the shelf were scattered on the floor. The photograph of Edward's friend or relative lay behind broken glass on the floor. Cushions from the sofa had been ripped open, and their feathers were strewn about. Here and there, an odd piece of the down clung to the curtains and the lampshade. Guy's cage had been overturned, and seeds spread around. The proud bird was not to be seen. Freddie looked around aghast.

"Edward," Freddie called out, filled with panic. "Edward, where are you? Are you alright?"

There was no response other than an intermittent hiss as if steam were being turned on and off.

"Bloody Hell!" he swore.

He hastily blew out the match and fumbled his way in the dark to the kitchenette to check there was not a gas leak from the stove. There was not. From here, the sound seemed further away. He struck another match. There did not seem anywhere obvious for the strange stop-starting hiss to be coming from. He concentrated on the sound and almost played the game 'hotter and colder'. The further away from the sound, the 'colder' he was and the closer to it, the 'hotter.' But this was not a children's game, far from it.

Groping his way through the darkness, striking first one more, then two more matches, he found the sound. It was under the table. He bent down, struck a third match, and crawled forward to look more closely. The matchlight flickered in front of him and reflected in two dark, fierce eyes.

"Guy, is that you?" Freddie questioned, confused.

"Hissss," the bird responded angrily.

Freddie reached forward to bring the parrot out from under the table and found that Guy was perched on what he had first taken to be a box but now appeared to be more of a boulder, a boulder of a man, huddled in a foetal position.

"Edward?"

The man-boulder responded with a shiver and a frightened whimper.

"Oh my God, Edward, what in hell's name has happened?" Edward cried out, filling time with words as his befuddled brain tried to make sense of what he had found in the cabin and what he would do about it.

Freddie put his hand on Edward. The old man shrunk further into his foetal ball and uttered nothing.

"Hissss," Guy defended his master and attempted to peck another vicious intruder, as he had done already that night, protecting Edward with his beak as best he could.

"Ouch!" Freddie gasped and raised his pecked hand to his lips to suck the pain away. "Bloody bird. I'm not going to hurt him. I'm going to help."

Slowly, patiently, Freddie cajoled Guy from under the table with seeds and soothing words and persuaded him back into his cage.

Edward lay still beneath the table. No longer shaking, he seemed to be soothed by Freddie's words and presence. With Guy safely away, Freddie could now reach his friend. Gently, he manoeuvred the old man from his hiding place and wrapped him in his arms. His clothes were damp and smelt of urine.

"It's alright, Edward, I'm here," he whispered as he cradled him, rocking him as a baby. "I'm here."

Freddie had no idea how long he sat on the cabin floor with the poor old man in his arms. His younger, violent self wanted to seek out the bastards who had defiled his friend and his friend's home and give them what for. He was furious at himself for not doing more - for not having identified those men in the pub. If indeed it had been them. He should find them. Do to them what they had done to Edward. But the man in him knew there were better paths of justice and that he needed to be where he was - on the floor of the cabin holding a man he loved, who stank of urine, as if he were a tiny child.

The dark sky beyond the cabin window lightened from purple velvet to lilac, and dawn's light began to banish the shadows of the night in the cabin. In the safety of Freddie's arms, Edward's body became less rigid, his breathing easier, and his skin warmer to the touch. After a while, Edward asked in a half-voice,

"Is Guy alright?"

"Yes, he's fine. I've put him back in his cage."

"Thank you," Edward replied. "He's a good old bird. He gave them some nasty pecks. They'll be left sorry today."

"Not sorry enough," Freddie replied grimly.

"I've had him a long time. He's been a good friend over

the years."

Now that the early morning sunshine was lighting the cabin, Freddie could see the magnificent red and gold bird that had been fashioned from grey shadow for the last few hours. Guy was asleep on his perch, worn out from the night's activities.

Edward tried to stand, but his legs were still shaking like jelly. As tenderly as any parent or lover, Freddie helped Edward to his feet and did all he could to help the old writer regain his normal state of cleanliness and neatness. As Edward dressed, Freddie got off the boat and cleaned the excrement from the paintwork. It was a vile job, and the stench made him retch. The people who had done this were disgusting and repulsive. But he knew it would be important to Edward that the outside world, the community in which he lived, saw a pristine, clean houseboat in the fresh light of the new day. He understood now how, for Edward more than others, what was on view must live up to the highest standards.

When he had finished, he made Edward a warming cup of breakfast tea while he did what he could to restore order to the cabin.

"Are you feeling better now, Edward?" he asked like a mother.

"Somewhat. Thank you, Freddie. I appreciate your kindness."

Freddie felt a knot of guilt. Helping Edward was the least he could do. Had he not been in some way responsible for all this? He picked up the books and returned them to the shelf, and instead of placing them at random, as would be his normal action, he arranged each in order of size from smallest to largest and in order of colour; green bound with green bound, red bound with red.

The photograph, which until that night had always been on the shelf alongside the books, lay behind the smashed glass of its frame on the floor.

"Who's this?" he asked, carefully picking the photograph out from the debris and placing it on the table in front of Edward.

"This is Alistair," Edward replied quietly.

Freddie disposed of the broken glass waiting for Edward to say more.

"It was Alistair who bought me, Guy, you know," Edward said. "He was hardly more than a chick then. We found him in a market in Cairo. He wasn't fully grown, but he was beautiful. Alistair saw how much I admired him and haggled with the stall owner, as is the done thing in North Africa, until both were satisfied with the price. We couldn't take the cage he was in as it was filled with the other birds, so Alistair bargained with the adjacent stall holder for this cage. That stall was a picture - piled high with carpets, ornaments in metal and wood, even musical instruments. Alastair was delighted with his gift. He was constantly buying me presents. He had the money to do that as his parents were wealthy and only had him to leave all their money to. I, on the other hand, have always had to write to pay my bills."

Alistair hadn't just bought the parrot and the cage. He had inserted a red patterned hearthrug and Arabian smoking pipe with green glass water bowl and silver stem into the bargain. The two young men giggled at the ludicrous sight they knew they made to passers-by as they returned to their hotel; Edward carrying a squawking bird and smoking pipe, Alistair with the rug slung across his shoulders.

"Our drawing room will be magnificent," Alistair said merrily. And indeed it was, once they had made the journey home laden with their luggage, a hearthrug, a pipe and a bird, across the sunny Mediterranean waters by boat, up from the heel of Italy by train to France, and then home to London.

"An Egyptian parrot, then?"

"No, I don't think so. He may well have started life further south. We don't always end up where we start."

"How did he take to life in England? Different from Africa, I dare say."

"He wasn't very impressed at first. Alistair and I lived in a cottage near Wimbledon Common. It was quite dark inside, and we couldn't let Guy out immediately in case he flew away. Later, after Alistair's father died and he received his full inheritance, we moved to a larger house on the edge of Richmond Park. Guy liked that much better. And by then, he had learned to return to us if we let him out of the cage and out of the window. We all liked it there. So did our friends. We used to have parties and soirées. There was always somebody visiting us - Laurence Housman, Charles Ricketts and Charles Shannon, you know, even Henry James came one evening, although he preferred to keep himself to himself."

"Do you remember that American writer Henry James, Guy?" Edward called to the parrot. "Do you remember those parties and dinners we had?"

As Edward talked, Freddie continued to tidy, silently making sense of the relationship and circumstances which were now being described to him. He was reluctant to ask questions, understanding that it was doing Edward good to think about his happy days and remove himself from the present moment where he had been so humiliated. But Freddie wanted to know. He wanted to know what had happened to Alistair and how Edward had come to live on the houseboat.

"Where was this photograph taken?" he asked, attempting to learn details without seeming to pry.

"At the Trevi Fountain in Rome. It was on our last holiday together. It was before the war."

During the day, they had visited the Spanish Steps and the Trevi fountain, appearing to the world as uninteresting middle-aged travelling companions. Alistair had posed next to the fountain, smiling for posterity into the lens of Edward's camera. Later, at midnight, in the velvety Roman darkness, they had snuck out from their hotel rooms and, holding hands, had walked through the shadows until they reached the fountain, where they kissed lustily. Alistair gripped Edward tightly, one hand on his head, the other across his back, reaching up to his shoulders. Edward placed one hand on his lover's cock and trailed the other in the fountain, feeling the water on his fingers in the pool and imagining the wetness he could make come into the other.

They could only steal a few moments so entwined before they heard the footsteps of another night walker approaching. Regretfully, Alistair released Edward from his embrace, and the two unremarkable English gentlemen proceeded to take the night-time air before returning to their hotel.

Later, Edward wrote the scene into a novel, replacing Alistair with Alison. It had sold well. But it was a lie, be it one that earned money, and he was never fully satisfied with the novel's success.

"You seem to have travelled a lot?" Freddie questioned as a comment once again.

"Yes, we did - Venice, Florence, Marseilles, Paris, Vienna. We visited so many lovely places before the war."

It seemed strange to Freddie, as he listened to the list of exciting and beautiful cities that Edward had visited, that there was no evidence in the houseboat of the travels which must have made up such a large part of his life. No evidence, that was, other than Guy, his cage, and the photograph of Alistair.

"Why did you stop visiting? Was it because of the war?"

"You could say that."

"But you were both too old to fight."

"But not too old to die," Edward said sadly. "Alistair caught influenza in 1919."

"I'm sorry."

"Thank you."

"Was that when you came here to the Lake District?"

"Yes, it was. I couldn't bear to stay in London and had no right to the house. It was Alistair's, not mine. A cousin claimed it. I wanted to be far away from all the memories of the life we shared and go somewhere where I could write. So I moved up here to the Lakes. First to Windermere, and when holiday makers became too intrusive, I had *La Speranza* moved to Derwent Water. I left everything behind. Everything."

"Well, it's very nice here," Freddie said. He wasn't sure what else he could, or should, say.

"Yes, it is. It has been - until now." A shiver went through his body as he spoke as if he had forgotten to take off soaking wet clothes and had suddenly remembered how cold he was. He looked down at the photograph of his Alistair in his hands, and Freddie saw his eyes brimming with tears.

"I'll have to get a new frame," Edward said - to himself, Freddie, Guy, Alistair, and the air.

As Freddie walked back to Keswick later that morning, he resolved to buy Edward that new frame.

****

Over the next few days, gossip about what had happened that night in the Nichol End marina travelled on the wind to Keswick and the lakeside hamlets. Most who heard the story had no inclination of what lay behind the outrage, and those that did, wisely or kindly, kept their mouths shut.

"Bad business with your friend the writer, Mr Booth," Mr Maddison commented to Freddie a couple of days later at breakfast at the Belle Vue boarding house. "May I ask you if he is alright?"

"Yes, he is fine now, thank you for asking, and yes, it is a bad business," Freddie replied, pausing his breakfast.

"It must have been city riff-raff," Mr Maddison continued.

"I expect so."

"You wouldn't get that sort of nonsense from any of the folk around here."

"No, of course not."

"But I do wonder, Mr Booth, what could have caused such an unprovoked attack on an old man and his property."

"I have no clue, Mr Maddison," Freddie lied. "But it is a very nice boat. Perhaps it was jealousy."

"No doubt," Mr Maddison nodded in agreement at Freddie's suggestion of a motive. "It's a shame we can't control the types we get on holiday up here nowadays," he continued regretfully. "But then again, we all need an income, and I benefit from the visitors as much as anyone."

Now it was Freddie's turn to nod in agreement.

"But it's a bad business, in any case. Do you think he might like some jam to cheer him up? I know Mrs French made a batch of raspberry jam yesterday. We could smell it all over the house, couldn't we?"

Freddie smiled at the remembrance of the aroma of the sticky sweetness.

"That's a kind offer Mr Maddison, but the ladies of Portinscale have given him enough of their own over the last few days to last him until next spring."

Freddie only came for two more breakfasts at the Belle Vue boarding house following the conversation with Mr Maddison. By the weekend, he had given his notice, packed his bags and carried them along the path from Keswick to Nichol End, returning a few hours later to make the same trip with the art supplies he had accrued throughout the summer.

It had been Freddie's idea to move into the houseboat with Edward for the rest of the season, and Edward had only resisted mildly. Even though Edward seemed on the surface to have recovered from his ordeal, Freddie knew that he was deeply fearful that the intruders, or others, might come back. Ever since he had held Edward in his arms on the houseboat floor, rocking him gently, he had felt a duty of protection towards his older friend. He had held the older man in his arms, touched his flesh, and had felt no revulsion for all that Edward was, only tenderness and sympathy. Gone was the angry youth, at war with the world around him, and in its place, there was now a man who was better than he had been before.

September brought golden sunshine to the Lake. Bright blue skies reflected in the water, rivalling each other for which could be the most azure. Red berries bejewelled the mountain ash at the side of the lake, and brambles offered up their harvest of blackberries for birds and man alike.

Freddie did not wander far from the marina. Finding peace and stimulation in setting up his easel close to the boats each morning and inspired by the rich late summer light, he experimented increasingly with his oil paints. As each day passed, his attempts progressed in Edward's evaluation from 'passable' to 'not bad' to 'really rather good'.

The end of September grew ever nearer. The date Freddie had promised his parents that he would return to London and do what was necessary to earn his living was looming as an unspoken shadow over them both. Freddie did not want to return to the capital. He did not relish the obligation to abandon his art and start work in an office, and he was still anxious at the thought of leaving Edward alone.

The day before Freddie was due to leave was filled with a heavy silence. Both men knew they would be the lonelier for their parting.

"Is there anything I can do for you before I go?" Freddie asked Edward as he packed his case the night before his departure.

"Yes, there is, actually."

"Oh good," Freddie looked up brightly, pleased that there was something that he could do.

"I'd like you to paint a portrait of Guy for me."

"Guy?" Freddie replied, full of surprise.

"Yes. Guy. I would like you to paint a portrait of my parrot, please."

"But I've only ever painted boats and views. I'm not sure I can manage a parrot."

"I'm sure you can. You are a better artist than you think."

Although the September light was fading, Freddie took out his easel, some blank canvas, his palette, his brushes, and his paint and quickly, as was his style, marked the outline of the magnificent bird before blending and smoothing the colours to bring the creature to life. He placed the red and gold parrot against a light summer blue sky and added some dark green foliage, which was not in front of him as he painted but seemed to compliment the parrot in his portrait. As Freddie worked, Edward turned on his gramophone and put on a record.

As the last bars came to their melodic conclusion, Freddie laid aside his paintbrush.

"Here you are, Guy. Do you like yourself?" Freddie asked the bird, turning the canvas to show him his painted self.

"Carrots! Mutton!" Guy squawked in appreciation.

"He likes it," Freddie said, much relieved.

"Of course, it's a good painting. Silly old bird," Edward said affectionately and stroked his pet on the back of his neck.

"I will write to you, you know," Freddie blurted out, feeling their goodbye was coming too soon.

"I'd love you to write. But what I really want you to do is paint!" Edward replied into the September stillness as he stroked his beloved pet parrot, and the water lapped comfortably against the side of his houseboat.

WINNIE

Anna held her worry tight to her chest. It was pinched close to her body, like the belted trench coat she was wearing. No matter where she looked, she couldn't find a place to rest her eyes. The landscape beyond the train window was either rushing past her too fast, forcing the moment she dreaded ever closer, or it disappeared from her gaze too slowly, making her wait interminable.

The carriage was freezing. Her coat was too light for late winter, but it was the only one that had fitted her slender frame. She would never have selected it if she had had the luxury of a choice. It was also why she was wearing a skirt when she would rather have been dressed in slacks. She yearned for the lost comfort of her uniform trousers. She had been lucky to get stockings with her demob coupons, but they were shocking, horrible knitted things that itched terribly. This new peacetime skin did not fit her, but she had to get used to it. Nothing about what she was wearing felt right. She crossed and uncrossed her legs, searching in vain for a restful position on her seat next to the window.

Her carriage had been full at Waterloo. Stop by stop, the passengers had reached their destinations and disembarked. Now there was only a tired-looking man, dressed in demob civvies, left in the carriage with her.

"Mind if I smoke?" he asked.

She shook her head and continued to look out of the window.

It was such a different journey, this one, to the last time she had taken this train, but the worry was just as real, just as tangible. And this time, she was alone, without Winnie.

"You look nervous," the man said to her. "Would you like a cigarette?"

Anna turned to look at him, surprised. God, yes, she would like a cigarette. She could smoke a whole pack. She was nervous. Terrified. Was it so obvious?

"Yes, please. Thank you."

She accepted one, taking it from the edge of his half-full pack.

"I've got a lighter," she said, reaching into her handbag to find the one that had lasted the war with her.

"No need," he said, striking a match, acknowledging her offer in the warmth of his voice.

They both lit their own. She with her lighter, he with his match.

They sat in silence, inhaling their cigarettes and blowing the smoke into their shared carriage, the motion of the train rocking them gently from side to side on the almost threadbare seats.

"Do you feel better?" he asked after a while.

Yes, she did feel better, slightly. She nodded.

"Where are you going?" he asked.

"Gillingham. And you?"

"Yeovil. What were you WRENS? WAAF?"

Her demob civies were as obvious as his own.

"WAAF," she replied. "Balloon barrages, and then when the unit was disbanded, I was posted to Suffolk - catering."

"Catering!" he laughed, not unkindly. "That's a bit different from balloons."

"I worked in a greengrocer's before the war, so I was at home with the vegetables."

She laughed now, and her face looked less pinched than before, the man noted. It was hard to tell how old she was, perhaps in her early twenties. There was no ring on her finger, he observed. Her dark hair and pale skin made her look a touch Irish.

"You're not going home, are you?" he asked. "You're not from Wiltshire. No Wiltshire lass has your accent."

She didn't answer. She took another puff of her cigarette. It was more than five years since she had left the East End. Since then, she had lived with girls from all over the country. She had slowly experimented with different accents and had settled on a home counties' elocution. She was not going back. Nothing was going to take her back.

"And you? What were you?" she asked.

He inclined his head slightly, acknowledging that she wasn't going to answer his question.

"Army. Devonshire Regiment."

"Europe?"

"Liberation."

Individual words conveyed a novel's worth of meaning.

They both turned their heads to look out of the train window at the wintery Wiltshire landscape.

"You know, I'm nervous too," he said after a moment.

He didn't look at it.

"Funny," he continued. "We buried all the nerves, didn't we? when Jerry was in sight when it was a case of surviving. But now there's no danger the nerves turn our legs to jelly."

He had finished his cigarette and took another from his pack. He held it out to Anna, and she shook her head.

"No, thank you."

"Ah, you're wise. I should follow your example. They'll last longer if I do." He put the cigarette back in the packet and tucked it into his coat pocket. His coat was thicker than hers, she noticed.

She looked at her watch. If the train was still running on time, then there were another twenty minutes before she would arrive at her stop.

"You'll be getting off before me," he said. "Yeovil's the third after yours. I haven't been home for more than two years. It will still be light when we get there. My wife will come to the station and bring the boys." He paused and sighed, "I just hope they recognise their Daddy."

Anna shivered involuntarily. His words were full of longing and fear. She couldn't say that his children would or wouldn't.

"How old are they?" she asked.

"Eight and five."

"A bit younger than Thomas and Henry."

"Thomas and Henry?"

"My nephews."

"Do they still recognise you?" he asked brightly, hoping that she had a good experience to share with him, to encourage him.

"I don't know. I haven't seen them since they were evacuated at the start of the war."

He looked crestfallen. He reached inside his coat and pulled out his wallet. It was battered and fastened with a strap and popper. She watched him open it up and take out a photograph. He looked at it fondly before offering it to her to look at. She didn't take it from him. She let him hold it out to her. It was a snap of a little boy and a toddler in their Sunday best, standing on a garden path, holding hands, smiling at the camera - smiling at their Daddy, smiling for their Daddy.

She'd only had one photograph of Winnie. Walter had taken it back in '38 when they had all gone to Greenwich for a picnic on the common. She'd kept it in her purse for years, but just before her posting to Suffolk, her purse had been stolen, and she'd lost her image of Winnie. It was like losing Winnie all over again. So she'd written to Ferne House, where Winnie was staying and explained how upset she was.

She hadn't been expecting anything from them. But then, one day, a small package arrived for her at the base.

Anna cried when she opened it. Tears of pain and pleasure as she looked at Winnie's serious, thoughtful face. Not a photograph but a painting oil sketch on a square of canvas. Who had painted it? She wasn't sure. Why a painting and not a photograph? She didn't know. But she was grateful, oh so grateful and wrote to thank effusively, sealing a couple of one-pound notes in the envelope with her letter.

"I hope Winnie will recognise me," she said. Her voice was so low that he could hardly hear it.

"How long since you've seen her?"

"Not since the start of the Blitz. I'm on my way to get her now. Take her home."

They sat in silence, nursing their nervousness, stroking their worries. The ex-soldier sighed again and put his photograph away in his wallet.

"I don't have a photograph," Anna said. "But I do have a painting. Would you like to see it?"

The man was surprised. Most people didn't carry paintings around with them.

"A painting?"

"Yes, it's in my case."

Anna's suitcase was in the luggage rack above her head. She stood up and took it down. Before the war, he would have offered to do it for her, but he knew better now than to offer such assistance to a WAAF, especially one who had spent years hauling heavy military balloons.

There wasn't much in Anna's case. Her underwear and a few personal belongings were at the bottom; the rest of her demob clothes were above, and at the very top lay Winnie. She picked her up and handed her to her travelling acquaintance.

He took the canvas square from her and looked at it closely.

"It's a dog!" he said in disbelief.

"Yes, Winnie's my dog."

"My God. I thought you were talking about your child or a niece, maybe. But a dog!"

Anna felt criticised. He must be laughing at her. She snatched the canvas from him, and he let go of it as he felt the force of her tug.

For a moment, the air was full of awkwardness and stale cigarette smoke.

"I'm sorry," he said. "I didn't mean to offend you. Please may I look at your picture again?"

Anna hesitated. She didn't want to present the picture, only to be mocked. But there was no derision on the man's face, only interest. Anna let him take the painting of Winnie from her.

A portrait of a little black terrier with a coffee-cream muzzle and amber eyes stared at him from the canvas. Its black nose seemed as shiny and wet as a real dog. The painted dog was concentrating on something it had seen and was perfectly still - waiting.

"How did Winnie come to be in Wiltshire?" he asked gently.

How did she, indeed?

****

It was the 4th of September 1939. The end of the summer, the beginning of the war, and the docks and roads were hot. The air smelt of water and expectancy. Walter had had work that morning. He was lucky, as he usually was. He was known to be a man who didn't shirk. He wasn't a troublemaker. He didn't drink. He didn't gamble. If he wasn't the first in the queue for the day's work, he was the second. He wasn't one to chat much to the other fellas. It wasn't that he was a loner. No, not at all. He was happy at the group's edge, adding a comment here and there if his words were of value and not if the conversation would put him off the task at hand, which was working to support his family - his wife Phyllis, his little boys Thomas and Henry, his sister Anna and her dog Winnie.

Today there were no words - no words spoken openly. But if angst were a language, there would have been conversations aplenty. There were whispers in huddles at the edge of the docks, in the alleyways of Limehouse, and inside the slummy and not-so-slummy dwellings. But there were no words out in the open. Nervousness was everywhere. Panic was rising higher and higher like thermometer mercury on a hot summer's day.

Hitler would strike and strike hard. The docks at the east of London would surely be his first target. Trade, the lifeblood of the British Empire, flowed through the port. It wouldn't be safe here. No one would be safe. But fellas like him had a job to do. The docks must stay open, boats with supplies must be able to land, and exports must be permitted to leave. He could face the danger. He would face the danger. But to allow his boys to stay in the path of the bombs? No. He could not allow that. They would have to go to the countryside where they would be safe from Hitler's malice, whatever Phyllis cried to the contrary. He'd been mulling it over all day as he worked silently, unloading the containers at the dock. The boys must go.

When his working day came to a close, he walked briskly back to the two small rooms he rented for his family in a tall, slim black-brick Victorian townhouse on the Commercial Road. It must have been a fine property in its heyday, but now it was shabby and over full. Its great attraction was that its last century owners had had plumbing installed. Walter's rooms were on the first floor overlooking the road. The rooms at the back were vacant since the previous occupant had died, but he was sure they wouldn't be empty for much longer. A large Irish family, the O'Malleys, were tenants on the ground floor, a family of German Jews, who had arrived bedraggled and fearful in '37, occupied the floor above them, and in the attic lived a family of true East Enders, like him. He picked up *The Daily Mail* from the stand on his way past, dropping his coin onto the counter, and glanced at the headlines.

Phyllis was standing at the kitchen sink washing dishes

when he entered. Henry, the baby, was in his highchair eating a slice of bread and jam. He had spread strawberry sugar around his mouth and cheeks, and sticky crumbs decorated his wispy hair. Thomas was playing with a wooden boat on the floor next to his baby brother. Anna and Winnie were not at home.

His wife turned to him wearily as he entered the room.

"Hello, love," he said, moving to take her in an embrace and kiss her. He felt her body tense and rigid under his palms. Always slender, since her last baby, she was reed-thin. When he touched her, he had the impression she would snap like a dry twig in autumn.

She shook him off.

"Phyllis, what's wrong, love?"

"I didn't sleep, the baby kept me awake, and I've had not a bit of rest all day."

"I didn't hear the baby,"

"No, I didn't let him wake you. I brought him in here with Anna. I put him back in his cot when he was finally asleep and then only managed an hour of kip myself before you got up and woke Thomas."

"I'm sorry, love."

He genuinely was. He knew how hard Phyllis was finding it looking after two little boys. Anna was not as much help as she could be, he acknowledged, but then neither did Phyllis try to make their home Anna's in a way that he would have liked his wife to have done.

He made to kiss her again, but she pushed him away for a second time.

"Don't. I've got too much to do. Just look at Henry. He's in such a mess. I've got washing out in the yard to bring in and the meal to cook." Her pitch raised with each statement as she began to work herself into a state of worry.

"I'll clean up Henry, love. Pass me a cloth," he offered to help.

Phyllis pinched her lips together and took a deep breath. She did not pass him the cloth.

"Come on, love. Let me help," he said.

"You shouldn't be helping," she blurted out. "You've been at the docks all day. Looking after the baby is woman's work. I can do it. I can look after my child. I can look after my home. I can. I'm just tired. That's all. Tired."

She sat down at the table and began to cry. Thomas, on the floor, was worried.

"Mamma?" he asked.

Phyllis reached for him silently and drew him to her lap, nestling her face into his soft toddler hair.

"I'll make some tea," Walter said. It was as good a proposition as any.

After putting the water on to boil on the stove, he wiped Henry's face, telling him what a handsome, good boy he was, and gave the baby two wooden spoons to play with, which the child banged on the highchair table in delight. Sitting on his mother's lap, Thomas was now pretending that the family table was the ocean and bobbing his toy boat on its high seas. The lads from the top floor came thundering down the carpetless staircase; Walter could hear their every step. Maureen and Douglas O'Malley, below, were yelling at each other again. Their swearing floated up through the floorboards, the soprano to the bass chord of the traffic on the Commercial Road drifting in through the open window. It all seemed like a normal day. But it wasn't.

Walter put Phyllis's tea on the table in front of her telling his eldest son to mind the hot cup. Phyllis hadn't moved, despite the list of chores she had previously recited.

This conversation was not going to be easy. But it had to be had.

"Phyllis, love," he said quietly.

"Yes," she replied, her eyes still shut, her head close to her child's.

"Phyllis, I've been thinking..."

"I know what you're going to say, Walter," she interrupted. "Why do you think I didn't sleep? It wasn't the baby. I lied. But I was relieved when he did wake up, I grant you, as it was better trying to soothe him than be wakeful, tossing and turning, worrying."

"We have to evacuate them," Walter said softly but firmly.

"No!" she snapped.

He was ready for this.

"We have to, Phyllis, sweetheart. It won't be safe for them here."

"It's not safe for any of us!"

"They're just little boys. They need to be safe. They'll be safe in the countryside."

"No. They're too young."

"Maybe you can go too. I heard that mothers are being evacuated with the little ones."

"No. I won't leave you. I won't leave here. This is my home. I can't be anywhere else."

Her eyes were full of tears. The limits of Limehouse were the limits of her world. The thought of leaving terrified her. Sending her children away terrified her. Keeping her children with her to be bombed in Limehouse, terrified her. She trembled on her chair - a wan leaf in a chill wind.

"Mamma?" Thomas asked, perturbed at his shaking seat.

"It's alright, Tom lad," his father answered, taking him from his mother's lap with a kiss and settling him on the floor at his feet. He pulled his wife gently into his arms in an embrace that she did not now reject.

"I'm not going to ask you, love," he said softly. "I'm going to tell you. The boys will go away somewhere safe, and you can go with them, or you can stay. But they're going."

He had hardly finished speaking before the little family could hear a familiar patter on the stairs and a well-known pawing at the door to their rented rooms.

"Winnie!" Thomas called out in glee.

"Hold on, Winnie," came a cheerful voice from the landing.

"Aunt Nana," the little boy called out in full-throttled joy.

"Hello, Tommy, boy," Aunt Nana called back to him from the other side of the door.

"Well, is no one going to let us in then?" she shouted through the wood. "My hands are full of vegetables, and Winnie can't open the door by herself."

Walter got up from the table and let in his sister and her dog.

His younger sister was bright and fun. She gave him her full grin from the threshold. Her thick black curls and pale, freckled skin made her look Irish, but Walter was unaware of any Irish blood in the family. She was laden with heavy bags, but it caused her no worry. Anna was as strong as an ox.

Winnie shot past their legs, making straight for Thomas. She gave her toddler friend a hello sniff and accepted a pat on the back before rushing, tail wagging, to the highchair to sniff the base and devour the crumby lumps of sticky bread the baby had dropped on the floor.

Phyllis rose from her seat to take the bags of vegetables from Anna.

"I don't know where you've been, Anna," she said crossly. "I've needed to start the meal this past hour, and you weren't here with the food. The children are hungry."

"Well, I'm here now, and I got extra," Anna retorted, immediately on the defence. "The carrots at the bottom of the sack were a touch mouldy, so Mr Mason said I didn't need to pay. He gave me the apples at half price too, and the potatoes. I got a quarter-pound more of the mutton at the butcher with what I saved."

Anna had a job at Mr Mason's Greengrocers. She'd started there as a scrap of a girl, running errands. Now she was trusted to sell the produce and stock the shelves. The few bob she earned wasn't much, but it helped with the family finances, and the remnant food she received in addition to her pay made an enormous difference to empty bellies, especially on the days, thankfully rare, when there was no work for Walter.

Phyllis said nothing. She took the potatoes out of the bag and started to peel them.

Anna sat down on the floor next to Thomas, and together they petted her dog. Winnie first lay on her side, accepting the strokes of her mistress and her little nephew. After a few minutes, she gave herself up to the full pleasure of the caresses, rolled onto her back, and spread her legs wide to offer them her stomach. The hair on her flanks was thick. Anna liked to push her fingers deep into it to feel the doggy skin below. By contrast, the hair on the stomach was thin; it hardly seemed to cover the dog's pink flesh. The tips of Anna's fingers reached Winnie's skin easily. She moved them lightly over the dog's belly, like a spider, like a pianist. Loose hairs detached themselves from Winnie's coat in the strength of Anna's caresses.

"That dog makes such a mess," Phyllis grumbled. "I'll have to wash the floor again when you're done."

Suddenly, Winnie stood up as if she knew Phyllis was cross with her. She scampered to the sofa in the corner of the room, which doubled as a bed for Anna. It seemed as if she was going to jump on it, but she stopped, turned round to look at Anna, almost to ask if she were allowed.

"No, Winnie," Anna commanded. Winnie crawled under the bed instead and busied herself, sniffing and pushing her muzzle into Anna's belongings.

"What are you looking for under there, you silly thing?" Anna called affectionately to her pet.

Phyllis, having finished peeling the potatoes, was now chopping them and throwing them into a pot. Old Mr Weiner was making his way slowly up the stairs to the floor above. They could all hear the sound of his walking stick and the Jew's unmistakable slow, shuffling steps.

Walter had opened the newspaper. He appeared to be reading quietly to himself, but he was thinking about all that needed to be done for the boys, who he needed to see, and who he could ask for help. They had no relatives in the countryside. The boys would have to go with the ladies from the Women's Voluntary Service. The ones who had come from the posh northern suburbs to rescue the East End children from Hitler. It would be best for all of them if he could persuade Phyllis to leave with the boys. Perhaps his entire little East End family could be lodged with a welcoming family in a cottage in the country? The naïve thought cheered him.

He turned the page. The rustle of the paper was almost as loud as Mr Weiner's feet. The headlines screamed war: 'Britain sets up war cabinet', 'Stand calm, united we shall prevail!', 'Gold must be sold to the Treasury', 'Rationing for petrol'.

Phyllis was now taking the carrots, mould bruised and white-whiskered, one by one from the greengrocer's paper bag. With each downward slash of her knife, she added to the pile of vegetable peelings on the table in front of her and added to her pile of worries. She wouldn't let Walter send the boys away. If there were bombs, they'd all go to the shelter together. Surely there would be shelters very soon? Was the basement of their house sturdy enough? It was full of accumulated paraphernalia, but perhaps the air raid wardens would say it was strong enough. Food. Good God! What would they do about food? There were bound to be shortages. The pile of peelings and worries grew ever higher.

With hardly a sound, Winnie darted out suddenly from under Anna's bed-sofa. In her mouth was a ball made from cloth and stuffed with rags. She dropped it next to Anna and then looked at her mistress with her serious, waiting eyes.

"That's where it went!" Anna exclaimed.

Winnie pushed the ball towards Anna with her paw.

"So you want to play?" Anna asked.

Thomas seeing the ball, abandoned his boat and hurried across to Aunt Nana and his baby brother. Anna lifted Henry out of his highchair, and all three, the baby with some help, took turns to roll the ball across the room and under Anna's bed. Winnie waited in utter stillness for the ball to disappear, and then she ran to retrieve it, bringing the ball back and dropping it at the players' feet. Soon the fabric ball became moist with dog saliva, which added to the game's charm.

"The problem will be food," Phyllis said out loud to no one in particular.

Walter looked up from the paper.

"It's going to be hard to get food," she continued.

"I'll still be able to get extra from Mr Mason," Anna said.

"That won't be enough," Phyllis replied with utter conviction. She could see the months ahead of them with complete clarity. "That dog will have to go."

"What?" Anna exclaimed.

"We can't keep the dog," Phyllis said, her pitch rising, her shoulders rising.

Anna sought her brother's eyes in a mute plea for him to intervene in the exchange and support her, his sister, rather than his wife. For once, he did.

"What on earth are you talking about, Phyllis?"

"There'll be little enough meat for us, let alone for a dog. We won't be able to feed it."

"I don't know what you're saying all this 'we' for," Anna grumbled. "Winnie's my dog."

"This is my house!" Phyllis shouted.

"It's not a bleeding house," Anna retorted. "It's two rooms in a house."

"I don't care what it is. It's still mine, not yours. We won't be able to feed the dog. It's got to go."

"You've never liked Winnie," Anna flung at her.

Baby Henry, sensing the tension, began to cry. Phyllis left her vegetable preparation and moved to pick him up.

"And the bombs, Anna," she said. "It's nonsense to take a dog to an air-raid shelter."

Walter had been silent since his first intervention. He watched Thomas continue to play with Winnie. The little boy wasn't bothered by the raised voices. Spats such as this between Aunt Nana and his mother were commonplace.

Walter felt tired, exhausted. He closed his eyes, and then he took a deep breath.

"None of us knows how animals will react to the sirens," he said.

"Winnie will be fine," Anna snapped. She grabbed Winnie when she returned with the ball and held her close to her breast, unconsciously reflecting the stance of Phyllis holding baby Henry.

"We don't know, Anna. We just don't know how Winnie will react. The sound could send her mad," he continued.

"She'll be fine. Won't you, Winnie?"

"I won't have that dog in my house. Not if it's mad. Not if it's eating food that the rest of us could have. Go on, Walter. Make her see I won't have it." Phyllis did not intend her entreaties to Walter to be mute.

"Anna," he said softly.

"No!" Anna cried, tears of anger and frustration biting into her eyes. "I won't let Winnie go."

"Well, if you don't do it. I will," Phyllis asserted.

"Do what?"

"Turn her loose."

"You can't do that, love," Walter said, momentarily siding with his sister.

Winnie, fed up with being held so tight to Anna's chest, no matter how much she adored her mistress, wriggled to be set down. Anna released her grip, and the little dog escaped to the floor and sat quietly by her feet, ears softly drooping, tail flat on the floor, perfectly still and of no interest to playful little boys. Her grave eyes seemed to suggest that she knew her fate was a silk thread held between the hands of the three adults standing in confrontation around the table.

"It would be cruel to turn her loose, love," Walter added.

"Well, then she'd better be put to sleep," Phyllis said as if it were a simple and logical way to remove the problem of her sister-in-law's dog.

"What? Kill her!" Anna hissed. "No, never. Not at all."

"Walter! Tell her. Tell your sister what she's got to do."

For the first time since he had returned that afternoon, his wife seemed calm. The tension in her face and body had gone. She had decided, and she was going to stick to it. On the other hand, his bouncy little sister was shaking in anger. Her eyes narrow, shooting venom in Phyllis's direction.

"Anna," he said wearily. "It would be cruel to inflict war on Winnie. Not when we all love her so much."

Anna could not believe what she was hearing. To love Winnie meant to destroy her? She turned her hatred to her brother.

"No!" she said icily.

"Come on, Winnie," she called. She strode over to the door, and Winnie followed obediently.

"Where are you going?" Walter called after her.

"Out!" she screamed, and she slammed the door so loudly that the frame shook so that the Irish family below, the Jewish family above, and the East End family in the attic could all be witnesses to her departure.

Anna flew down the stairs, Winnie chasing after her, relieved to be away from the shouting but not sure why they would be going out again when they had only so recently come home. Mary-Louise O'Malley and her sister Hannah were sitting on the front doorstep. There were so many O'Malley siblings squeezed into the downstairs rooms of the house that they frequently spilt over into the hall, the doorstep and the minuscule front yard. They parted, one little girl leaning to the right and the other to the left so that Anna could make her way through them and onto the street.

"Hello, Nana," Mary-Louise grinned at the young woman from upstairs.

"Sorry, petal, I'm in a hurry," Anna apologised, and she turned abruptly left, away from the house and in the direction of Shadwell.

Winnie was not in such a rush and paused to sniff and nuzzle the two little girls on the doorstep. Neither one was wearing shoes or socks; they rarely did. Winnie drank in the scent of childish toes and gave a friendly woof before she scurried away from them to catch up with her mistress. She soon overtook Anna and ran ahead to explore a pile of boxes left in a doorway, a rubbish bin at the side of the street overflowing and needing collection, some faeces deposited by another dog close to the curb, and various lampposts on which she detected others had left their signature. Winnie ran from left to right on the pavement in front of Anna, as if determined to trip her mistress up.

"For goodness' sake, Winnie!" Anna rebuked her crossly. Words that Winnie ignored.

The Commercial Road was busy. Traffic flowed in both directions - cars, vans, buses. Anna and Winnie passed shops and businesses, homes, and cafés. The great artery of the docklands had never struck her as being peopled with pets, but today she saw them everywhere; cats lurking in alleys, stroked by passers-by on doorsteps; dogs following their owners on leads or their owners following them, or sniffing the streets alone, maybe strays. She had never noticed how many animals were part of the city's life.

When she arrived at Mr Mason's grocery shop, she was

out of breath, and her fury was high. She rang the doorbell. She banged on the glass pane of the door front.

"Anna, what's wrong?" Mr Mason asked as he let her back into the closed shop. She had not long left. It wasn't like her to return so soon.

"Mr Mason," she cried, "I've got nowhere else to go. They want to kill Winnie."

Mr Mason was silent - he'd been expecting this. He nodded slowly.

"You don't agree with them, do you?" she cried out, hardly believing that the only person who she trusted other than Walter, who had now shown his true colours, was also going to desert her in her hour of need.

"No, Anna. It's not right," he said, and then he sighed. "The government says it's kinder to put pets to sleep than to let them suffer in air raids. There's a pamphlet about it. Not that I've seen it mind, I only heard about it this afternoon when you were out back. The message will get into the papers too, no doubt."

"But this is terrible!" Anna cried. "Hitler hasn't got a war with pets, has he?"

Anna was eighteen years old. Sometimes, she was as mature as an old-married lady with a brood of children; sometimes, she was no more than a little girl.

"Anna, in war, we have to do what we think is best for the community, and also what we are told. You can't take food from the bellies of children, can you? To feed to an animal?"

"I don't want to listen," Anna shouted and made to leave the shop. "I thought you would help me."

"I will help you, Anna," Mr Mason said calmly. "If you like, I'll keep Winnie here with me until this all blows over."

"Do you think it will?"

"Undoubtedly! This pet business is little more than a storm in a teacup. I can't say the same for the war, though. That'll be bad. When it comes."

Anna smiled her thanks, and her body released its tension. She bent down to Winnie, rubbed the little dog's black head, and stroked her back, trying to explain to her beloved pet what would happen. But Winnie did not understand, and as Anna left the shop, the little terrier strained to follow.

"No, Winnie, you're to stay safe with me," Mr Mason said sternly.

Winnie looked at him askance. Mr Mason never spoke to her with such authority. She was used to him and his shop; she came here daily with Anna. But she was never left behind here without the mistress she adored. She pawed at the closed shop door and whined as Anna walked determinedly away along the Commercial Road back in the direction of Limehouse.

Mr Mason was as good as his word. He hid Winnie in the yard at the back of his shop. He turned a packing case on its side to give her a makeshift kennel. Anna came to work every day as usual and cuddled and caressed her dog out at the back, but Winnie was not allowed into the shop to see and sniff the customers or to leave the premises and go out onto the street. At the end of the afternoon, the same performance was repeated for seven days in a row; Anna hardly bearing to say goodbye, Mr Mason commanding Winnie to stay, and the poor little confused terrier pawing at the door and whining as the woman he loved walked away, abandoning her, day after terrible day.

But Winnie was safe. Thousands weren't. In a blanket hysteria, animal after animal, pet after pet, was euthanised in a week of slaughter - a national shame, a knee-jerk reaction of panic at the onset of total war.

Nothing was said back in the first-floor rooms. Walter had persuaded Phyllis to leave for the country with the children, and there was a flurry of activity to get the little family ready. Two days later, Walter put his tearful, anxious family on a train at Marylebone destined for Buckinghamshire with a dozen other families, all in the care of a couple of middle-aged, mild-mannered W.V.S. Five days after that, Anna brought her dog home. She could live with Walter, but she was not sure she could forgive him. Their two rooms reeked of stale silence.

****

The winter sky had been slowly greying as the train made its way westward. The clouds had become thicker as Anna told her travelling acquaintance her story. Almost imperceptibly, sleet began to fall. Slashes of ice were caught on the carriage window and forced to travel on the train before melting into water drops and escaping from the glass as rain. Anna shivered. She was cold in her thin coat. There was nothing she could do about it other than run her hands over her arms to warm them and gently pound her feet on the carriage floor to encourage her blood to surge around her body.

The ex-soldier, who had been listening attentively, took out his Woodbines again and offered her another cigarette. This time she didn't refuse.

"I'd forgotten about the pet cull," he observed. "Bad business."

He breathed the cigarette's nicotine into his lungs, where he held it, before exhaling the fumes thoughtfully. This young woman intrigued him. Here she was, recently demobbed in February 1946, having experienced all the different dangers of war and having made all the usual sacrifices, yet, her passion remained with the injustice of an incident in September 1939 when the whole country had, in his opinion, been a little 'touched' in the head. He wondered what had happened to her family.

"So, you said your sister-in-law and nephews were evacuated to Buckinghamshire. Where exactly?" he asked.

"A place near Stowe."

"It's nice there."

"Is it? I don't know."

"You didn't visit?"

"No. Too expensive to get to."

"Did they stay there all the war, or did they come home before the Blitz? Lots did, didn't they?"

"Phyllis went out with the boys at the beginning, and they all stayed with a family with a spare room in their house. But it didn't work. Phyllis didn't like the way the woman cooked the food, and the woman felt that Phyllis ought not to be criticising her, as she came from Limehouse, which isn't exactly heaven on earth, is it?"

The man smiled to himself. Now he understood her home counties' accent.

"She was going to bring Thomas and Henry back to the docks," Anna continued. "But she heard of a children's home opening up for the babies near Buckingham, and she got both of them in there. It meant she could come back to Limehouse. She didn't like the country, and Walter needed her to work."

"Work?"

"Yes. The landlord put the rent up. We needed every penny. With men leaving for war, there were packing jobs going at the warehouses. She got a place with a tea merchant."

"And you? What did you do?" he asked with interest.

"I stayed working with Mr Mason until the Blitz. By then, I'd had enough, so I joined up."

The man had finished his cigarette. He ground the stub beneath his heel on the carriage floor and left it alongside the ones he had already smoked during this last section of his journey. He picked up the little painting of Winnie that he had placed on the seat next to him when he had reached into his breast pocket for the cigarettes. He concentrated on her soft, sober expression. He felt that he wanted to tickle her on the crown between the ears and make her smile, if dogs can smile.

"And Winnie?" he asked. "What happened to Winnie? I feel as if I know her."

The Blitz had happened. That is what had happened to Winnie.

****

The summer of 1940 had been so hot. Unbearably hot, with temperatures in the 90s. The fruit and vegetables withered and rotted quickly at Mr Mason's grocery store despite the electric fan he used to cool the shop and the awning which gave shade to the front. The war was on holiday, but the docks were still at work. Boats from the Empire and carriers from the Americas made their way safely in and out of the port. The booms of their horns echoed through the docks and along the river Thames.

Phyllis's prediction had not come true. There was enough food. There were no bombs. Walter's wife and sister reached a mute and silent truce. At first, Winnie missed the little boys, but the Irish children from the ground floor gave her plenty of attention, so Thomas and Henry soon faded into a pleasant dog memory.

The planes arrived from the east. It was 5 pm on a hot and lazy Saturday afternoon. Saturday 7th September. Black

Saturday. They glinted silver in the afternoon sunshine. Yes, they were seen, but they were believed to be British. The RAF on manoeuvres. Anything else was unfathomable. The destruction the German planes wrought was equally unfathomable.

The sirens shrieked. They wailed and moaned.

Anna was in the street with Winnie and the Irish children. The youngest, Betty, began to cry. Big sister Hannah, ashen-faced, grabbed her little sister and tried to take her back into the building to find their mother, but the parents, their faces full of panic, came running from the house with gas mask boxes grabbed in haste. Footsteps pounded on the stairs as the inhabitants of the upper floors rushed to vacate the building. Old Mr Weiner descended at a speed he'd never demonstrated before, caught up in the fast current of escape, carried in the tide of his family and neighbours.

On the pavement next to Anna, Winnie trembled from head to toe. The noise of the sirens was terrifying. The worried faces, the calls of fear, and all the people she knew from the house running away from the building as if it were already on fire confused her. She shook and whined and butted her head against Anna's legs.

Anna picked Winnie up and held her close to her chest. She ran, following her friends and neighbours to the basement air raid shelter three buildings along. She held tight to her dog. She clung to the Irish family. At nineteen years old, she was hardly more than a child herself and not much older than the oldest O'Malley.

The dark basement was crammed with frightened neighbours. Some knew each other well, and others had never said hello to each other the whole time they had lived on the Commercial Road. Anna looked around for Phyllis and Walter. They weren't there. They had gone out for the afternoon. If Anna had known how to pray, she would have prayed that they had made it to a different shelter in time. And Mr Mason too. She willed with all her might that he would be safe as she held Winnie tight in her arms, her whimpering, terrified baby. Nobody spoke. They listened in dread to the sound of the sirens above ground, the crash of bombs falling. The children who had been crying buried their faces into their mothers' skirts and stifled their sobs. Only Winnie did not know how to be silent, revealing her fear to all in a high-pitch whine and crying yelps.

"Can't you make that bloody dog shut up?" a man shouted angrily.

Anna didn't reply but drew Winnie tighter to her chest to smother the sounds.

"It's a bit bloody stupid to bring a dog down here, isn't it?" the same voice criticised.

"I'd say it is!" a woman from the other side of the basement joined in. "No one else has brought a pet in here. We might be in here for hours. What if your dog goes mad?"

"Leave her bloody well be!" Douglas O'Malley stepped in to defend Anna. "The dog's here. We're all bloody well here. The dog's no more terrified than the rest of us. She just doesn't know how to keep it in."

The woman's eyes shone as huge black coals in the dim light in the basement. Working herself up into a panic, she cried,

"The dog might go mad and bite us!"

"We've got more to worry about than a dog," a quieter voice in a soft foreign accent added. It was Mr Weiner. The weight of his words ended the basement debate on Winnie's right to shelter.

In the corner of the basement that the Irish family had secured for themselves when they arrived, Anna whispered,

"Thank you, Mr O'Malley. I couldn't have left Winnie behind. I couldn't have left Winnie alone up there."

"No, lass, you couldn't have."

Yet plenty of owners had done just that. Wilfully abandoning their pets to their fate or simply forgetting them in the face of their own.

The below-ground hours had been long, each minute burdened with waiting, fearing, hoping. With Winnie safe, Anna's only thoughts were of Walter, Phyllis and Mr Mason. Evening turned to night, and the name of the hour became irrelevant to those trapped together in safety. Anna dozed fitfully, huddled alongside Hannah and Mary-Louise O'Malley. When the all-clear was sounded, Anna and her air-raid companions left the shelter in a daze. Above ground was a disfigured city. The immediate area of their basement shelter was untouched, but within eyesight, what yesterday had been homes, warehouses, and shops, were now piles of dusty rubble. The largest fires were still burning, and exhausted firemen struggled to contain the Luftwaffe's destruction. The shelterers breathed a sigh of relief that their patch was unscathed.

Anna hurried back to the townhouse. Winnie was in no such haste. Relieved to be back above ground in the daylight, the terrifying sounds of yesterday now eerily absent, she was almost her old self, investigating as many new and old exciting scents on her way as Anna's quick steps permitted, almost exhilarated by the change to Limehouse that the bombs had wrought. When she reached the staircase to their first-floor rooms, she bounded up the stairs ahead of Anna. The door to their rooms was ajar, and she pushed it with her crown just enough to squeeze in. Anna followed, opening the door fully.

Although the building itself was undamaged, the tremors from the bombs had shaken the few pictures that the family owned from the walls and the handful of books they possessed to the floor. The plates that had been drying on the draining rack before the carnage commenced were no more than china fragments on the floorboards. Oblivious to the disorder, Walter and Phyllis sat covered from head to toe in dust, drinking tea at their kitchen table as if it were a typical Sunday.

"Oh good, Anna, you're safe," Walter said, genuinely relieved that his sister had returned unscathed, but in his shell-shocked state, he could not summon any more enthusiasm at her entrance.

Phyllis, staring with unfocused eyes at the wall in front of her, sipped her tea. She put the cup down on the table.

"Shame that the dog is," the woman said almost under her breath so that it was hardly more than a voiced thought.

It took three full seconds for Phyllis's words to reach Anna's understanding. Her white face became paler, and her eyes narrowed in contempt. The concern she had had for Phyllis's safety evaporated and was replaced in an instant with cold hatred for the woman who was casually sipping tea as if today were a day of rest or a bank holiday.

Winnie, relieved to be home and in familiar surroundings, had shot under Anna's bed and into the dark comfort of a place that smelt of Anna and all her possessions.

"Come on, Winnie," Anna called.

Winnie had no intention of leaving now that she was back at home.

"Come on, Winnie," Anna commanded, a knife blade entering her tone, cutting through the air and Winnie's resistance. "We're not wanted here."

A little black nose poked itself out from under the bed, and a body swiftly followed.

Anna walked out of the door without saying goodbye.

"Anna, where are you going?" Walter called after her. "Where are you going, Anna? Please. It's not safe to go out and not tell us where you are going."

"To Mr Mason's to check he's alright," she shot at him over her shoulder.

Fires were smouldering all around. The air was thick with ash and death. Anna hurried along the Commercial Road in the direction of Shadwell, tears streaming down her face. Winnie ran along behind. Nothing diverted her attention now. She dared not let Anna out of her sight.

Mr Mason's grocery was standing, but the glass had been blown from the windows. The shops, further along, had not been so fortunate. Skeleton structures of twisted metal, fallen bricks and burnt wood were all that was left. Anna shivered. She hoped the people who lived and worked there had made it out.

Mr Mason was in his grocer's beige overalls as if it were a normal shop day. He had already swept up the broken glass and was now carefully checking that there were no splinters amongst the fruit and vegetables he still hoped to sell. His mind, though, was hardly on the task. The door was not locked. Anna entered, followed by Winnie, the bell at the hinge announcing their arrival.

"Anna!" His anxious face lit up. "You're safe. Thank God. I've been so worried."

She didn't respond but stood like a limp rag, the fight taken from her, in the middle of his shop, surrounded by sales bins of potatoes, apples and pears.

"What's wrong? It isn't Walter and Phyllis, is it?" He was quick to imagine the awful scene of her family wiped out.

She shook her head. But the stress and strain, the fear and the exhaustion of the last hours overwhelmed her. She let it flow from her in sobs that shook her body. Mr Mason put his arms around the young woman who was almost his daughter.

"There, there, Nana dearest," he soothed. "There, there. You're safe. We're all safe."

"I can't go back," she sobbed.

Mr Mason listened. He understood. He put it to her that she had options. He didn't want to lose Anna - she was a good worker - but there was a queue of others to take her place. She could join up. Become a WREN or a WAAF. In his opinion, it wouldn't be long before conscription would be extended to include young, single women, so she might as well join first. She wouldn't be in any more danger in the services than she was already in living in the East End. If she'd had enough of boats, then why not give her talents to the Women's Auxiliary Air Force?

"No," Anna asserted. "I can't leave Winnie."

"Anna," he said sternly. "When you're called up, you'll have to leave her."

"But what will happen to her?" Anna wailed. "Can you look after her? I'll send you money from my pay?" she clung to a glimmer of hope.

"I've got a better idea than that."

He went into the small room at the back of his grocery shop and returned with a newspaper. He opened it up on the counter. 'Lady Hamilton's Piece of Peace for Pets,' she read. The article explained how Nina, Lady Hamilton, a passionate animal-lover, appalled by the pet cull of the previous year, had opened her country home at Ferne House in Wiltshire to pets in need. Pets who needed shelter from war, pets who needed a home whilst their owners fought in the war.

"Pet evacuation!" she grinned at him, her pale, tear-stained face lighting up with the first genuine smile he had seen on her face in many months.

"Exactly!"

The bombs fell thick and fast. Young people were sucked into the military effort and were spat out all over the country, all over the world - Anna included. Mr Mason helped Anna write to the sanctuary at Ferne. He helped her find the words to paint her situation: she was an orphan; she had joined the WAAF and was leaving soon for training before being posted goodness knew where in the kingdom; when she left, Winnie would be homeless, as much an orphan as she was herself. Please, would they take her? Lady Hamilton's staff wrote by return of post and said yes.

Anna felt sick on the journey to Wiltshire. She had never travelled so far from London in her life. Her world was changing with every mile that the locomotive took her from the city. Fear sat in her stomach and tried to escape from her throat. Worry made her fidget in her seat until the stern eyes of a soldier in uniform, an officer sitting opposite, forced her to stillness.

Winnie sat on the floor by her feet, tucked behind her ankles and sheltered by the carriage seat. She felt her mistress's anxiety. Now and again, she nuzzled at Anna's shins, stood up, turned round in a circle, sniffing her spot in the carriage, and sat down again. She looked out at the travellers who boarded and dismounted with her sad, amber eyes. Again and again, Anna lowered her hands to Winnie to tickle her crown and pat her side.

"It's alright, Winnie," she assured. Herself or the dog?

The guilt weighed heavy on her. She was about to abandon Winnie and did not know when she would see her again. But at least Winnie would be safe and well-cared for. She pushed the echo of Thomas and Henry's departure from her life to the recess of her mind, refusing to recognise the parallels or to submit to the guilt of disinterest in her nephews. All she felt guilty about was Winnie.

****

"Pet evacuation!" her travelling companion of today shook his head in astonishment. He would not have believed it if he had not heard it from the lips of this ex-WAAF and seen the miniature oil painting of her dog.

"What's it like at this place - Ferne Manor, was it?"

"Ferne House," she corrected. And added with a smile, "It's heavenly. There's so much space for the animals. They've been well cared-for. Lady Hamilton is a saint of a woman."

She must be, he agreed.

"Did she save many pets?"

"Hundreds for sure, maybe thousands."

"Thousands!" he whistled and shook his head. Thousands. That was really something.

If Ferne House had been a refuge for Winnie through all these last long years of war, it had been Anna's salvation. Knowing that her dog was no longer in any danger from people or bombs, she had been able to throw herself into her postings in the WAAF, working hard, making friends, doing her bit. Changing her life. Cutting her ties with the East End.

There was still more to tell. The incomplete narrative sat between the ex-soldier and the former WAAF like a piece of music that finishes at the penultimate bar and does not return to the home key for the final chord.

"What happened to your brother and his wife?" the man asked.

Anna's face clouded, and she dropped her eyes to the floor. He had seen expressions of this kind over the months and years of the war, and it always meant the same thing.

"Walter was killed not long after I left. A direct strike on where he was working when the raids were still in the day rather than the night. I couldn't get to his funeral. I'd only just joined the WAAF and was denied leave."

"I'm sorry," the ex-soldier said. And he was. He really was.

"And your sister-in-law?" he pressed.

"I've not heard from her much. She's still in Limehouse. She'll never leave. I heard from Mr Mason that she married another docker last year."

"And the boys?"

"I think they're with their mother," she replied vaguely.

He nodded his head in sympathy, trying not to judge. He had no right to judge. He handed the painting of Winnie back to Anna.

"I should have that framed if I were you," he suggested.

She nodded and put the painting back into her case. There were not many minutes left of her journey.

"Thank you for the cigarettes," she said to him as she stood up, tightened her belt, and made herself ready to descend with her luggage. She looked at the cigarette butts on the floor and wondered if she should pick them up and take them with her or leave them for a train cleaner.

He followed the direction of her eyes.

"I'll deal with them, don't worry," he said.

"Thank you…" she stopped. "I'm sorry, we've been chatting all this time, and I never asked you your name."

"It's Jeremy."

She put out her hand to shake his goodbye as the train drew to a halt at the little country station.

"And you?"

"It's Anna. Thank you, Jeremy," she said.

He stood up and pulled the window down so he could put his hand through it and open the door from the platform side to allow her to get down from the carriage. Sometimes it was the polite thing to help an ex-WAAF.

Anna left the train and, turning back, she said,

"I'm sure your boys will remember you."

He nodded. Yes, they probably would. He shut the door.

Jeremy watched as Anna began to walk towards the station's exit. He imagined he understood her fears for the future. The train started to pull away slowly. In a swift move, he stuck his head out the window and shouted to the young woman on the platform,

"Anna!"

She turned to look back at him.

"Winnie will know you, don't worry."

She smiled in thanks.

"And Anna - make it up with Phyllis. The boys need you."

The train was picking up speed, so he couldn't see how his words were received. He shut the window and lit another cigarette, alone with his thoughts in the carriage.

PERCIVAL

PERCIVAL

They hadn't planned to go to the art show. They'd planned to go for a walk on the other side of the county, which they didn't usually visit, where their 'guide to local walks' book informed them that there was a pretty village with an excellent pub for lunch. Dave had decided it all the evening before. The boys didn't come with them, of course. The bribery of a delicious roast was not enough to get them out of bed on a Sunday morning to join their parents. Their plans trumped those of their parents these days. Chris had just passed his driving test and was going to take Emily's car so he could see his girlfriend Tara, and Leo had arranged to play computer games online with his classmates. So, Dave drove Emily to the pretty village, Emily feeling a pang of regret at the absence of noisy boys in the back.

The pretty village of Ayot St Lawrence was not as they expected. Through the winding lanes, they'd noticed temporary signs to the art show staked into the ground. They had thought little of them. It couldn't be much, an art show in a church. But when they arrived at the village, there were cars and people everywhere, and all the parking spaces on the road outside the pub were taken. Emily began to feel anxious. She felt the day she'd expected begin to slip away from her, and she never felt relaxed in a place which she didn't know. At least Dave was driving.

It didn't worry Dave too much that there wasn't a parking space. He was more concerned that the number of cars would mean waiting for roast lunch, or worse, no lunch.

He turned the car around at the end of the village and retraced his route to the temporary car park in the field next to the church. It was already half full of vehicles. A team of boy scouts with yellow neon safety jackets was directing new arrivals. A lanky teenager indicated that they should take a space near the exit. When Dave had parked, Emily got out of the car and began taking off her shoes to change into her walking boots. Dave held back. It wasn't possible to see the church through the trees that separated it from the field car park, but he could hear voices from that direction. Other visitors were hurrying from their parked cars in haste, making for the art show. It gave Dave the feeling that he was missing out, and he hated to miss out. He thought it would be a pity to ignore the attraction, even though art was not his thing.

"Are you coming?" Emily asked, wondering why he wasn't beside her by the boot, preparing himself for their walk.

Dave stood by the driver's door and turned his key over in his hand thoughtfully for a couple of seconds, and then he looked at his watch. It had just turned 11 o'clock, and his stomach rumbled on cue.

"Maybe let's not change into our boots just yet, Em? Why don't we go and have a look at the art show?"

Emily looked at him blankly. They'd come for a walk and lunch, hadn't they? Not an art show. That wasn't part of the plan he'd set before her for today.

"I bet there'll be coffee and cakes up there," he added suggestively.

She looked down at her summer shoes and at the field, which wasn't too muddy despite all the recent June rain and agreed with him that it was time for a mid-morning snack.

"We'll look at the art, grab a coffee and a bit of cake, come back, change our shoes and go for our walk. Perhaps we'll stop off at the pub first and find out if we need to book a table. If the worst comes to the worst, we'll have an early lunch and then do our walk, or we'll go for our walk and come back for a late lunch." Dave was planning it all out. Emily merely had to go along with it. They held hands as they walked up the lane from the field car park to the church, Dave leading the way.

A smiling volunteer sitting behind a table at the entrance marquee asked for their £2 admission fee and gave them a glossy catalogue listing all the artists and paintings in return. Some of the pictures had been reproduced in tiny thumbnail colour print. Emily squinted at it. She'd have to put her reading glasses on to look at it more closely if she could be bothered.

"Have you been here before?" the visitor-greeter asked.

"No, we haven't," Dave replied.

"Oh, well, you're in for a treat," she responded. "The show's been running for over 40 years. It's quite an event!"

"I can see," Dave nodded appreciatively.

"We have over 80 artists exhibiting. Not all of them have their work on panels as there's not enough space in the church, so please take a look at what's on the tables in the marquee. There are cards and postcards for sale too. And if you go through to the end, you'll find the tearoom in the smaller marquee."

"Thank you," Emily and Dave both said in unison.

The air smelt of freshly cut grass and coffee. There was the pleasant sound of happy chat and activity ahead of them. Dave breathed it all in and took Emily's indifferent hand.

"Come on, Em, let's look at the paintings and then get some coffee."

They walked past the tables of art and the boxes of cards.

"You'll want some cards, won't you?" Dave said, glancing only briefly in the direction of the card stall.

"Probably," Emily mumbled, pulled along in his wake.

They went up the stairs to the church, unaware of the glorious view behind them across Hertfordshire fields. The pew-less church was a vast, high-ceilinged, 18th-century cavern. Display boards, crammed with paintings of all sizes, lined the walls and had been arranged to create rooms within rooms inside the ecclesiastical space. Even though it was before lunch on a Sunday morning, the show was busy. It was a gallery with art to admire. It was a shop with art to purchase. It was a fundraising event to support the church. It was something to do on a Sunday morning before lunch.

"The paintings with the red dots have already been sold," a man's voice said to them from their left.

"On the paintings?" Dave queried.

"No, not on the paintings themselves - on the name

signs below," the man explained in a friendly and welcoming way. Emily began to feel more at ease.

"Have many sold?" she asked.

"Yes, quite a lot have since the show opened on Friday evening. But there are still some left. If you like what's already gone, you could always contact the artist and find out if they've got any others. All the artists are listed in the catalogue," he added, waving the copy in his hand. Emily raised hers and looked at the cover, which was indistinct without her glasses.

"Oh, that's good," she said. She would never read the catalogue, but she had to say something in response to the friendly remark.

There seemed to be an unofficial one-way system to view the paintings, with visitors starting on the left and moving clockwise around the room. Dave and Emily joined the circuit.

The art on display was eclectic and mostly very easy on the eye. There seemed to be no order to how the paintings were hung, with the genre, size and artist all mixed up in a free-for-all marketplace. There were paintings of seascapes and country lanes, pictures of flowers that looked like flowers, and designs that did not. There were acrylics, watercolours, collages, pen and ink and computer-generated prints. And there were animals, lots of animals - wild, domestic, British, and foreign. There was something on offer to suit everyone's tastes.

Emily moved almost mechanically across the width of

each panel. Some of the paintings appealed to her, and then she commented, "That's nice" or "This one's good." Dave did likewise. Mostly they picked out different items, and occasionally, they agreed on the same. It didn't matter. It was only something to say. They weren't going to buy anything. The art show was entertainment before their coffee and their cake.

She didn't notice the painting at first. It was only the size of an A4 piece of paper, and it was almost hidden by the surrounding seascapes and pastoral views, yet it called to her. She stopped dead in her tracks. A tiny tremor of excitement ran up her neck. Against a bright turquoise background, a cream and beige sheep stared vivaciously out at her from its frame. It had bounced full of life into the painting from the side. The artist had not placed the sheep carefully in the middle to create a self-congratulating portrait of British countryside idyll or land-owning wealth, but had allowed the sheep to catch him by surprise, jumping into the frame - 'Hello, I'm here' - the sheep leapt into the picture and into Emily's life.

Emily was transfixed. She was nailed to her spot by the unexpected energy in the painting and the friendly, lively expression on the animal looking at her as if it wanted to know her, as if it wanted to be part of her unlively and uneventful life. She looked for its name sign and red sticker. With an unexplainable feeling of relief, she saw no red dot. No one had bought the sheep.

She reached into her handbag for her glasses. Now she could read the sign easily. Number 82 'Percival,' it said. Who would call a sheep Percival? She thought as she looked up number 82 in her catalogue. Peter Wilkinson, the artist, would. He would call a sheep Percival and would price it at £175.

Dave, who had got ahead of her in the unofficial one-way system, made his way back to Emily. He was surprised to see her wearing her glasses and looking in the catalogue.

"What have you seen?" he asked.

"Percival," she said, pointing at the sheep.

He looked at it, not particularly impressed.

"Percival! Who'd ever call a sheep Percival?"

"Peter Wilkinson."

"Who's that?"

"The artist."

"How much is it?"

"£175."

He pulled a face as if he had sucked a lemon. "That's a bit steep for a sheep," he winced and moved on.

Emily reluctantly said goodbye to Percival. Dave hadn't liked him.

But as Emily moved around the room, Percival watched her. Emily felt him. If Percival could have bounced out of the frame and down from the wall, he would have followed her around the church as the little lamb followed Mary. Emily didn't see any more of the paintings. They were all a blur. "Yes," she replied to Dave's comments of "That's nice," or "This one's not too bad," or "I don't like that one." She kept turning her head back to look at Percival. When a family stopped to look at him, she felt a wave of panic rise from her stomach. What if they bought him? What if a child persuaded a parent to buy the bouncing sheep? It was precisely the picture a child would like, want, and might get.

"Come on, Em, let's have some coffee," Dave said to her as they reached the end of the one-way circuit.

"Did you like anything?" the man at the door asked them.

"There's some great art there, but nothing that's for us, thank you," Dave replied for them both. "We're going for some coffee and cake now."

"Enjoy!" the man said pleasantly. "I can recommend the carrot cake, but the Victoria sponge is also to die for."

Emily was silent and followed Dave reluctantly down the steps. She left the painting of Percival behind on the panel in the church, but she imagined she heard the light clatter of four hooves on the concrete steps behind her. The lamb following Mary.

Someone with great artistic talent had transformed the marquee from a tent into an attractive tearoom appropriate for an art show. The tables had been covered first with bright amethyst fabric cloths, which hung down low, and then with smaller white plastic ones placed on the diagonal, easy to wipe down for the next set of tearoom guests. In the centre of each table was a simple white vase containing fresh flowers - glorious bunches of purples, pinks, creams, and greens - arranged as if a gardener had picked them from her garden and placed them almost carelessly in a spare vessel. No florist here had arranged the blooms within an inch of their floral lives.

A table laden with homemade cakes ran the length of the end of the tent. There was almost too much to choose from, not just the recommended carrot cake and Victoria sponge, but ginger cake, chocolate brownies, shortbread, lemon drizzle, coffee and walnut, scones and jam, and flapjack. Every art show visitor would be able to find their favourite. Dave bought a large slice of gooey chocolate fudge cake to accompany his coffee and a chocolate brownie for Emily to have with hers.

Dave commented on the tearoom as they ate and drank. Then he speculated on the age of the church and today's church attendance. He got into a conversation with an older couple sitting at the adjacent table who were local and knew the village well and were surprised that Dave and Emily had come from the other side of the county. Emily stayed silent, thinking about Percival, feeling the lamb underneath the table at her feet gently nudging her, wondering if the boys would like him as much as she did.

"Are you alright, Em?" Dave asked when he had finished his conversation with the occupants of the next-door table. "You're very quiet today."

"Yes, fine. I was just wondering about buying some cake to take back to the boys," she said.

"Lazy gits!" he said affectionately. "They don't deserve it. They should've got out of bed and joined us."

"You wouldn't have done at their age," Emily defended.

"No, you're right. But my mother wouldn't have bought me cake as a reward for not getting up. Em, you've got to stop treating them like they're little boys. They're young adults now. They make their own choices."

Yes, she thought, they do. They choose to spend the afternoon with their girlfriend or play online games with the friends they see every day of the week at school. At least buying them cake was providing for them and reminding them that their mother was still there. Always there.

"They'll always be my little boys," she laughed, turning the serious into a joke, buying her sons their favourite slices, and taking them away in two little paper bags.

Dave left the tearoom marquee ahead of her. She felt his irritation that she was doing something that he had opposed. He strode past the steps up to the church, making his way to the exit.

The magnet inside the church was powerful. Emily could feel its pull as she tried to follow her husband. It caught her in its grasp. She turned her head to look into the church and could just about make out the panel where Percival was hanging. She couldn't go. She couldn't leave him.

"Are you coming, Em?" Dave called impatiently. The first part of his plan was complete. It was now time to move on to their walk and their lunch.

"I'd like to look at that painting again," she called back, rushing up the steps before he could stop her.

There was still no red spot at number 82. Emily's shoulders slumped in relief. She couldn't go without him. Percival had called to her from the painting. He needed her. She needed him.

"Oh, come on, Em, you don't want that do you?" Dave said in irritation from behind her.

She didn't reply.

"Emily, it's a sheep. Why do you want a picture of a sheep?"

"I like it," she replied simply.

"But where would you put it?"

If there wasn't space for it in the house, it was pointless owning it was his subtext.

"In the bedroom?" she suggested.

"No!"

"In the dining room?"

"No! I won't look at him and eat my dinner. What about the downstairs toilet?"

"No!"

Now it was her turn to protest, but at least he was cooperating on wall space, she noted.

"And it's expensive, Em, £175."

"That's not bad for an original," she said.

"How would you know?"

She thought quickly and waved the art show catalogue at him,

"You can see from the brochure it's quite in line with other prices, better even."

She didn't know that. She hadn't looked. She was making it up because she couldn't go home without Percival.

"You really want it?" he asked.

"Yes, I do."

He stood silently for a moment, looking from his wife to the painting and back to his wife, holding his breath while he decided what they would do. He then let it all out in a huff of irritation. Buying a painting had not been on his agenda.

"Looks like you're coming home with us, Percival," he said to the painting. "Percival. What a name. You'll have to come up with something better than Percival, Em,' he added as he made his way over to the friendly man at the entrance to find out how he should pay for Emily's painting.

"You're lucky," she heard the friendly man say to Dave. "I'm surprised the little sheep didn't sell on the first day. Wilkinson's work is very popular. It normally flies off the walls. He's one of our most sought-after artists. Maybe you and your wife were meant to have it."

"Maybe," Dave replied through gritted teeth.

****

Later that afternoon, Emily felt a warm feeling of satisfaction as she hugged her wrapped-up painting tight after taking

Percival from the boot of Dave's car following his journey to his new home.

Chris was as unimpressed with the sheep as his father, but Leo liked him. She hung the painting in the sitting room, taking down a print of a boat in the harbour where they had been on honeymoon and replacing it with Percival. The school photo portraits of the boys on the sideboard below almost seem to be gazing up at him. The two lads and the sheep all looked as cheeky as each other and made Emily smile.

"Is it alright here?" Emily asked Leo anxiously as he entered the room, eating a slice of chocolate spread on toast, using his hand for a plate.

"Yeah," he mumbled, scattering crumbs on the carpet. He swallowed his mouthful and wiped his chocolate lips with the back of his hand.

Dave was sitting on the sofa, scrolling through his phone.

"Do you have to?" he asked.

"What?" Emily jumped, thinking he would add, "Hang it there." He had objected to every other place she'd suggested but hadn't commented when he must have seen her remove the boat in the harbour.

"Drop crumbs, Leo," Dave clarified sharply. "You make too much work for your mother. She'll have to vacuum up after you."

Leo ignored his dad, instead offering his mother a

chocolatey kiss to apologise for the crumbs, which she hungrily accepted.

"Do you think the artist painted Percival from his imagination, or do you think he's a real sheep?" Leo asked, examining the painting in its new home on their sitting room wall.

Real or imagined? Imagined or real? The scales of Emily's opinion tipped in favour first of one, then the other, then back again, before they settled.

"He's got to be imagined. Sheep don't look like that," was Dave's opinion from the sofa.

"He looks like a sheep to me," Emily defended.

"You've had so much to do with sheep that you know?" Dave mocked.

His sarcasm riled her, and before she knew it, she was defending herself.

"No, you know I haven't had 'much to do with sheep'," she said. "But he's got that long sheep face and poking out ears."

Emily knew she wasn't describing Percival to the best of her ability. But somehow, it wasn't what he looked like that appealed to her; it was his character - a character that had to exist to call to her in the way it had.

"I think Percival's a real sheep," she said quietly, knowing that her son and her husband had already lost interest.

Now that she had decided that Percival was more than a painting, she couldn't leave that thought in a frame on the wall. She had to know for sure, and there was only one way to find out. She would have to ask the artist himself.

She felt Percival nudging her, pushing against her shins with his head. "Go on, Em," he seemed to say. "Go and find out."

"Alright," she smiled. "I will."

Peter Wilkinson had conceded to have his name and studio address in Essex printed in the art show catalogue, but Emily couldn't find his contact details anywhere, and he did not appear to have a website.

"Go on, Em," the sheep at her knees seemed to say. "Go and see him and find out."

"But I can't," she whimpered. "I can't drive to Essex! I don't know the way. I'll get lost."

Driving made Emily anxious. She only ever drove where she knew, where everything was familiar. So how could she get there? Dave wouldn't take her as he'd think the idea was a waste of time. Chris was out with Tara all day and night now that he'd finished his A-level exams, and he wouldn't help her. She'd ask Julie, she decided. Julie would help.

Emily had known Julie for the last ten years. They met when Emily started a part-time job at Marks and Spencer's when the boys went to primary school. It had been Dave's idea as the hours suited the school day. It wasn't a demanding job. She had to think, but not too hard. She enjoyed serving customers and was glad their problems were not particularly complicated to solve - issuing refunds or finding alternative sizes. It was fun when the new ranges came out until she'd seen them for four days a week, month after month, and she became indifferent to them. There had been quite a change of sales assistants over those years, but a core of five was still there, Julie and herself included. Julie was older than Emily. She had taken the job as something to do when her youngest had left home, and finding that she enjoyed 'doing' in a shopping centre, she had stayed and planned to stay until she retired or until the shop closed down, whichever came first.

"It's a bit crazy!" Julie said, obviously delighted at the prospect of a day off that did not consist only of cleaning and shopping.

"I know," Emily confessed with a giggle, feeling like a teenager with a madcap plan.

"Don't tell Dave," Julie advised.

"Why not?" Emily asked, a cloud passing over her face and bringing with it her troubled look, which was at home on her features.

"Oh, just that he'd probably tell you not to go because it wasn't his idea, and that would be a shame because we're going to have a great time."

Peter Wilkinson's studio was in a village that had once been an island in the countryside but was now a suburb of the local town. At his address, a black cat sat on the red brick garden wall and mewed a greeting or a warning at them. Emily paused to say something to the cat but thought better of it. She followed Julie up the driveway and waited silently beside her friend for someone to answer the doorbell. No one came. The plain red brick cottage seemed hard and austere as if no one was in or wanted to be in. Perhaps that was what the cat had been telling them.

"We've got to speak to Peter Wilkinson," Emily began to wail. "We've come all this way. We can't go back without talking to him." The bag with the painting of Percival, which she had bought with her, seemed to hang uselessly by her side.

"I can't see why he couldn't have a phone number or an email address," Julie said - and not for the first time. She saw her friend's anxious face and quickly returned to the positive. "Maybe he's round the back? And if not, we'll leave a note, go and find some lunch, and come back in a little while. We're in no rush."

There was a gate at the side of the cottage that had been left not fully open or fully closed, and although not exactly inviting them into the back garden, it wasn't barring their entry either.

"Mr Wilkinson," Julie called out. She made her way through the gate.

For an artist's house, the garden was strangely bereft of beauty. There was an old swing set with flaking blue paint and a handful of roses doing their best to bloom on spindly uncared-for bushes. There were a couple of pots of herbs by the back door, which had been attended to, but no geraniums or other summer bedding that a garden centre or a corner shop could have easily provided. There was plenty of grass, though, which had been freshly mown following the recent summer rain.

"Mr Wilkinson?" Julie called again.

The two friends could hear the faint sound of radio music coming from a building at the end of the garden.

"Maybe it's his studio?" Emily suggested, hopefully.

They followed the path to a building that must have been built as a garage with access from the lane at the back. It was no longer fit for purpose since one side was piled with boxes - an overspill of possessions from the house, and the other side was crammed with canvases, boxes of paintings, paint tubes and brushes. It was hard to believe that anything as gorgeous as Percival had been created in such a shabby surroundings.

The door was open; inside, a man stood painting at an easel. Julie knocked on the open door and called softly, "Mr Wilkinson."

He turned around nervously.

"I'd hoped you'd go away," he said.

"Excuse me?" Julie replied, somewhat taken aback.

"I heard you at the door and hoped you'd go away. I don't like seeing people," he continued, and he turned his back on them and resumed painting.

He wanted them to go. He couldn't focus on painting while these two strange women stood at his doorway. He pretended to be concentrating on a dark patch in the corner of his canvas.

Emily, not to be put off, moved closer to the easel. It was a painting of a black cat on a red brick wall.

"Is that your cat?" she asked.

"Yes," he replied abruptly. And then, softened by curiosity, he added, "How did you know?"

"We saw the cat outside your house," Emily responded gently. Now that she had secured his attention, she didn't want to lose it.

The cat in Peter's canvas was calm. It was a waiting cat, a sedate cat you could trust to be at home when you returned from your day's work. Yet its green eyes sparkled with mischief as if to say, "I might be here when you get home, but you've no idea what I get up to you when you're away."

"I've known cats like that one," she said. "What's his name?"

"*Her* name," he stressed. "It's Rhona."

"That's an unusual name for a cat," Julie said. It reinforced her opinion that Peter Wilkinson's names for creatures were of his style.

"Why are you here?" Peter asked sharply.

Emily could feel his anxiety and recognised it as a sibling in herself.

"I bought one of your paintings at an art show, and I wanted to learn more about it," she said gently. "It's such a lovely picture. I admire your skill. Percival is a very special sheep."

Her tone soothed him. As she spoke, she took her painting from her bag and held it out for him to see.

"Ah, Percival!" he exclaimed, putting down the brush and taking back his creation. "How are you, Percival? Is this woman looking after you?"

He seemed surprised when the painted sheep did not respond. And indeed, Percival, full of life, did look as if he ought to be able to baa his answer from the picture frame.

Peter looked at the woman who had handed him the painting more closely. She was no longer an irritating presence but a person who had empathy with his world. He wasn't very good at judging ages or circumstances, but he could see the essence of a character in a glance, and in front of him, he saw a quiet woman waiting, waiting like Rhona, the cat, for a chance of a bounce in a life like Percival's.

"Did you paint Percival from your imagination, or is Percival a real sheep?" Emily asked gently.

"I always paint the animals I know," he replied. "Percival belonged to the landlord at the Three Brewers in the village."

"Belonged?" She queried, a tremor of desperation entering her voice. The euphoria of having been correct - Percival was a real animal! - slipping from her grasp at the thought that she might be too late. He might no longer be here.

"Belonged - belongs, I don't know. There was some sort of bet, and the landlord, Tony, ended up bottle-rearing an orphaned lamb in the spring before last. Percival was definitely at the pub a few months ago when I popped in, but Tony told me then he'd have to go as the Brewery weren't pleased about having a sheep on their property. The powers that be thought it better if Percival was on a farm. Tony's wife was quite upset about it. She'd taken to Percival."

Peter handed the painting back to Emily.

"Nice sheep, Percival. Quite perky."

"So, it wasn't you who called him Percival?" Julie asked.

"Me? Of course not. Stupid name for a sheep!"

Emily and Julie left Peter in his garage studio with his painting of Rhona and made their way into the village to find the Three Brewers.

****

It was no quaint village pub in a timber-framed building. It wasn't a cottage where villagers had drunk together for centuries. It didn't look like the place where two middle-aged women would stop for lunch together on a day out. The Three Brewers had been built in the 1970s or 1980s when the village had been significantly extended. Its flat brick front was spectacularly ugly, despite the effort to cheer it up with a hanging basket of geraniums at the entrance and some unfortunate slug-nibbled Busy Lizzies in boxes at the ground-floor windows.

Nothing about the day was how Emily had expected. She stood in front of the pub feeling sick and disoriented as she once had when she had stepped off a fairground ride with the boys when they were little and had vowed that she would never repeat the experience, no matter how much they begged her. But the story of Percival waited for her inside, even Percival himself, perhaps. She felt her little lamb nudge her from behind, pushing the backs of her calves. "Go on, Emily," he seemed to say. "Go on in and find me."

"Come on, Emily," Julie echoed, pushing the pub door open and entering. She held the door for her friend and added gently, "It's going to be fine. You'll see."

Not being old and not being particularly big, the pub was full of daylight. It was a venue with an identity crisis. As if to remind the clientele that a pub in a village should be the harbinger of rural heritage, there was an enormous cartwheel, somewhat dusty, attached to the wall close to the bar. On the opposite wall, dark iron horseshoes had been mounted to create a large W shape. Yellow-brass cowbells and a couple of brown pottery jugs viewed the room from high-up shelves. Mixed into the rural paraphernalia were photographs of the local football team and posters for events long passed that meant something to somebody, either because the event had been special or because the poster's images remained attractive.

The lunchtime trade had scarcely started, and there were only half-a-dozen customers in the pub. There wasn't anybody behind the bar.

"Excuse me," Julie called out, craning her neck to try and see into the kitchen at the side.

A round-faced man with round glasses and a round belly

came out.

"Hello," he said cheerfully. "What can I get you?"

Emily was lost for words. 'Percival', she thought. "A glass of white," was what she said.

"What would that be?" he asked, sliding a wine list over the brown wood bar top for her to select her geographical preference - France, South Africa, New Zealand.

Oh dear, now she would have to get her reading glasses out of her handbag. She felt stupid, really stupid. Why was she on a wild goose chase to find a sheep? A childish picture of a sheep. A childish woman who didn't want anything to change but was desperate for something new. Her hand trembled as she undid the bag's clasp to reach inside for her glasses.

Julie, standing alongside her, ordered half a Guinness. She'd have liked more, but she was driving.

"Emily?" she asked. Emily knew that the question did not mean "What are you having," but "Well, aren't you going to ask him about Percival?" She felt the young sheep's forehead push impatiently against her hand on the clasp of her handbag.

"I'm looking for a sheep called Percival," she ventured, her nervousness making the words sound sharp and unfriendly, not at all easy-going and cheerful as Julie or Dave would manage.

The man's sunshine expression disappeared instantly. He hadn't recognised these two women as locals. Now one of them was asking about his sheep. He knew he should have sorted the problem out. This meant trouble. Tony wasn't sure whether to feign ignorance or say nothing. He chose the latter and served the half-Guinness in silence.

"Is Percival still here?" Emily tried again.

Still, he did not reply to her question.

"Have you chosen what wine you'd like, Madame?" he asked. Knowing full well she hadn't.

"A glass of the cabernet-sauvignon," Julie replied on Emily's behalf, referring to the bottles she could see in the fridge in front of her rather than the list on the card.

"I'd really like to know about Percival," Emily repeated.

She felt like she was going to cry. She could hear her voice come out as a wail.

"Please, I've got to know. Is Percival here? Peter Wilkinson said he thought he was."

At the mention of the artist's name, Tony began to relax. If these women knew Peter, they couldn't be from the Brewery or DEFRA, that government department that managed farms and the environment.

"So, you know Peter, do you?" he asked, buying himself a little more time.

Tony breathed a sigh of relief. He could smell not a whiff of the Brewery or DEFRA.

"Odd fellow, Peter, isn't he?" Tony said, still not quite ready to share Percival with the strangers.

"Definitely!" Julie agreed heartily.

"He's made quite a business with his animal paintings, though. That's one he did of my dogs a few years ago," he said, nodding toward two Golden Labradors frolicking on a sunshine-filled patch of grass. The painting was nestled in the right-hand V of the horseshoe W, and neither Emily nor Julie had noticed it.

It was very nice, Emily thought, but it was not Percival.

"And Percival?" she asked.

Tony ignored her.

"I'd have thought an artist would be a bit better with people," Julie commented, taking a sip from her Guinness.

Tony had now poured Emily her wine. The liquid was chilled from the fridge and a hint of condensation formed on the glass.

"Yes, he does tend to hide himself away. He had a wife once, I believe. I think she left."

"That's all very interesting, but please tell me, is Percival still here?"

Emily was surprised at her assertiveness. She hadn't come all this way to talk about an artist. She didn't care whether Peter Wilkinson had a wife or not.

"I'd like to know the sheep in my painting," she said, looking straight at Tony, not averting her gaze as she so frequently did in the face of confrontation or intensity.

Tony made up his mind, and his sunshine expression

reappeared.

"What would you say if I joined you and told you all about him?" he asked, reaching for a dark bottle of Malbec on the shelf behind him and pouring himself a glass of the musky red.

As he drank, he told them he'd had puppies that had become dogs, kittens that had grown into cats, kits that had turned into rabbits, and a daughter that had transformed into a woman. He explained how he'd got a bit drunk the winter before last with a mate up in Bury St Edmunds and boasted he could raise a lamb. His mate said he couldn't. He bet he could. He'd thought nothing more of it until late in the night a few weeks later, in early March, he got a call from his mate saying he'd found him a lamb to raise. It belonged to a farmer with a capsule flock - sheep not being the thing in East Anglia. The mother had died giving birth to the lamb, and the lamb seemed weak, not likely to last. It was probably going to die. Probably better that it did. All rather stupid. But a bet's a bet, and he was sad at the thought of the lamb not having a chance. So, he said yes, he'd try his hand at raising the lamb and promised his mate and the farmer that he'd complete all the DEFRA paperwork.

Alison, his wife, was unimpressed at first, but she got up early the following day to go with him to Bury to collect the lamb. The baby sheep might have been small, and his odds not so great, but Alison and Tony took one look at him and knew that he would make it. Life was meant for him, and he was going to live it. They took him home and bottle-fed him. Had they any idea how much a lamb feeds? It was hard work! And my goodness, did they know how strong a baby sheep was, sucking the bottle with force to rip your arm off? Nothing like bottle-feeding an infant.

Emily thought of her baby boys and laughed.

"Hungry baby boys can be a bit like that."

She was enjoying herself. She felt more relaxed now, listening to Tony's sparky and almost improbable story.

"Did you keep him in the house?"

"Yes, at first. But he's moved out to the garden now."

"Peter said he thought you'd got rid of him."

"Not yet, but we do have to find him a new home," Tony said regretfully. "You see, I said I'd do the paperwork, but I forgot. You're not meant to transfer livestock from place to place without telling DEFRA. Some civil servant somewhere thought it would be a good idea to inform the Brewery that I had an unlicensed sheep living at the pub. The big bosses weren't too keen about that when they found out and told me the sheep had to go. He can't go back to the farmer, as he's sold his flock. He's a great sheep - such a character. He's outgrown here. He needs to move on to a new home. But I guess I'm just reluctant to let him go, bottle-raising him as I did."

Emily understood. She nodded.

"Can I see him?" she asked.

"Yes, of course. He's out the back. I can't go with you, I'm afraid, I've got to stay in the bar, but you're both welcome to go through."

Julie had been silent throughout, listening carefully and sipping her Guinness until only a centimetre of brown liquid was left in the bottom of her glass.

"Was it you that called him Percival then?"

"Yes. Cool name, isn't it?"

She hastily swallowed the half centimetre so as not to have to answer.

Throughout Tony's story, Emily could feel the sheep sitting obediently at her feet under the table, like a well-trained dog, becoming increasingly impatient. It raised his right hoof and tapped her on the lap. Then he did it again and again. "Go on, Emily," it seemed to be prodding her. "Go on out into the garden and find me." When the two friends stood up, she could feel it leap ahead of them, its bottom bouncing up and down in haste as it ran, leading the way to the real Percival.

The back of the pub reflected the front, stark and ugly, despite the pots of garden-centre bedding on the terrace and the shrubs planted at the edges of the lawn to soften the angles. The bright red sun umbrellas sprouting from wells inside the heavy wooden table benches and the purple flower cones of the buddleia joined the pots in an attempt to bring what beauty they could.

At the end of the pub garden, a wooden partitioning had been erected to create a pen. Emily hurried to it. Julie was pushed to keep up. Apart from grass, the only thing inside the pen was a shed on the left-hand side. Emily's anxious eyes swept the space.

"Percival," she called out, "Percival."

The pen seemed deserted.

"He's not there," Emily moaned, desperately disappointed.

"Hold on," Julie touched her arm and drew Emily's attention to the shed.

From around the side of the shed, a perky cream and beige face with pointy ears was looking at them inquisitively.

"Percival," Emily called.

"Baa," Percival replied, and he scampered over to greet them. Not at all shy, he wondered who the two strangers could be.

He was utterly the sheep of the painting. Peter Wilkinson had captured his character on canvas, and Emily already knew him.

"Hello," a voice called up the path from the house. Emily and Julie turned round to see a woman in jeans and a white summer blouse approach them.

"I'm Alison, Tony's wife. He told me you were out here. So you've met Percival. Hello Percival," she added, reaching over the fence to pat him on the head and tickle his crown as if he were a cat. Percival loved the attention, pushing his forehead affectionately into Alison's palm for more.

"He didn't seem scared of us," Emily said.

"No, he's grown up around people, living in a pub as he does. They say sheep can recognise up to 50 different faces. He's certainly got used to a lot of regulars at the Three

Brewers."

"So, is he like a pet?" Emily queried. It seemed strange to think that a farm animal could be so domesticated.

"Yes, I guess you could say that," Alison agreed. "I think Percival's special, though. He's very friendly and curious."

"Isn't he lonely?" Julie asked.

"He doesn't seem to be. But sheep are flock animals, so maybe he'd be even happier with other sheep. We'll know soon enough when we've managed to find him a new home."

Emily put her hand down into the pen. Leaving Alison's caresses, Percival moved to Emily's hand, which he sniffed and then nuzzled and licked. The same tingle of excitement and expectancy that Emily had felt when she first saw him at the art show travelled through her neck as he touched her in the flesh now, as he had touched her in the heart then.

****

"No!" Dave said crossly later that evening. "No, Emily, absolutely not! We are not having that sheep here."

Nothing she could say about how cute and friendly Percival was or how much he needed a new home made any difference to Dave's refusal to consider her proposal of Percival coming to live with them in their garden. She didn't say how much she wanted Percival, how much she needed Percival. Dave ought to know that. He ought to be able to see that.

"You didn't even tell me you were going there," he grumbled, as much offended by her doing something without telling him as by her wanting to do something he hadn't suggested.

Leo was playing on the computer with his friends when she asked him his opinion.

"Yeah, Mum, that's great," he said.

"You think so?" she queried, rather shocked he'd agreed.

"Yeah, it would be great to vibe with a sheep."

Sometimes she didn't understand her fifteen-year-old son.

"So you think it's a good idea?"

"Yeah, I do, Mum. Can you go now? I'm playing."

He hadn't taken his eyes off the screen.

The next day, Chris was planning on playing tennis with Tara in the park and couldn't wait to tell her the latest news.

"You'll never believe it," he said as soon as she opened the door.

"What?"

"Mum's planning on getting a sheep!"

"What?"

"A sheep."

Tara liked her boyfriend's mum; she was kind, gentle, and unthreateningly ordinary.

"What's she going to do with a sheep?"

"Keep it as a pet."

"How can she keep a sheep as a pet? People don't have sheep as pets."

"Mum seems to think they do."

"Where's she going to put it?"

"I don't know. She's still arguing with Dad about it. Somewhere in the garden, I suppose."

"What does she want a sheep for?"

"I don't know. I can't see why she can't get a dog. Other parents get dogs."

"Especially when their kids leave home," Tara agreed. "She probably wants a sheep because you're going to uni."

"But a sheep, Tara. Everyone will think she's mad. I wish she'd get a dog."

"She'll be lonely when you're gone," Tara continued, warming to her theme. "It won't be the same having just Leo in the house."

"Well, I guess they look a bit similar. They could pass for brothers," Chris said impishly.

"How so?"

"Percival and Leo both have long faces, curly hair and pointed ears."

The pair dissolved into giggles.

****

With a determination that Emily did not realise she possessed, she got ready to welcome Percival to her home. Dave had reluctantly agreed - very reluctantly. But when he came round to the idea, he decided that the plan was entirely his. He read up on keeping sheep as pets. He worked with Leo to build a pen at the end of the garden under the trees and in front of the bank. It was where the boys had had a climbing frame when they were little. Now that they were teenagers, the frame still stood, a forgotten piece of junk in the shade. Dave dismantled it piece by piece and took it to the recycling centre. When it disappeared from their view, it was hard to remember that it had ever been there.

The middle of the new pen was open to sunshine and was filled with lush grass, but the sides and the bank were shaded by overhanging branches and never seemed to dry out after a rainy spell. It was a patch of the garden where not much grew except assorted fungi and nettles. Dave had never been able to do much with it. It might as well be a pen as not, he conceded, as he filled out the DEFRA paperwork for his wife's new pet sheep.

Several times a day, Emily looked at Peter Wilkinson's painting of Percival on her sitting room wall. Each time she felt a flush of excitement and nervousness. Was this what new parents waiting to adopt their chosen child felt like? she wondered. Alison sent photos of Percival daily on her phone, and Emily replied with messages of thanks on hers.

Julie found Emily a large dog box for the car to fetch Percival. It was second-hand. She cleaned it out carefully so it didn't smell of dog and scare the sheep. Julie would have liked to return to the pub with Emily to collect Percival. She liked Tony and Alison. It would have been nice to have seen them again. But now that the plan to rehome Percival had become Dave's project, he had claimed that job for himself. He chatted easily and freely with Tony and Alison when he arrived, ever so interested in all the details of Percival's history, the problems with DEFRA and the brewery, what it was like running a pub, the plans Tony and Alison had for their next holiday. Emily listened to the conversation while she played with Percival, her soon-to-be pet, patting him and talking to him.

She was worried that Percival would not take to his new home, that he would be an unsettled toddler at nursery crying for his parents, refusing to leave the dog basket, cowering fearfully at the side of his new pen. She need not have worried. When she set the dog basket down on the grass, the same long perky face, pointy ears and curious eyes reached out as they reached into his portrait. He lowered his head to sniff the ground and taste a blade or two of green grass. Then he walked brazenly into the centre of the pen and made his new home his own. Emily sat with him outside for the rest of the day, leaving her men to find their lunch and only remembering at the last minute that Leo needed to have his dinner made for him before Dave dropped him at a party in the evening.

The next morning, she opened the curtains of her bedroom window to let in the bright new day and looked down into Percival's pen. She could see him lying on his side, dozing and smiled softly to herself at the thought of her sleepy sheep. She got dressed and glanced out of the window. He was still on his side, fast asleep like her boys in their bedrooms, dead to the Sunday world.

Dave was already up. He had gone for an early morning walk to the newsagents to buy the heaviest Sunday edition on offer that week. He had announced the night before that he planned to read in the morning, fix the dripping bathroom taps in the afternoon and that he'd booked them both tickets at the cinema for a film he knew she didn't want to see in the evening.

"Percival's having a good sleep," he said to her as she entered the kitchen. He'd already had one cup of coffee, and there was at least another waiting in the cafetière in front of him.

"He's probably exhausted from his move yesterday," she responded, thinking fondly of the previous day's adventure.

Emily opened the back door to go out into the garden to say good morning to Percival. It had rained during the night, and the August air was warm and damp.

"I'm not sure he should be on his side," Dave added before taking a sip from his coffee.

"Really? Are you an expert on sheep?" she teased lightly, remembering his recent words to her.

"Well, I read that sheep ought not to be on their side. It's normally a sign of something wrong."

She looked at him in alarm. Was he being serious? If he was, why was he sitting so calmly drinking coffee and reading the Sunday paper if something was wrong with her sheep?

"Only saying," he added, lowering his eyes back to the

table to continue reading the article he had been perusing when she entered.

Emily ran to the pen. Percival hadn't moved. He was still on his side in the same position as she had noticed from her bedroom window. His fleece was wet with the rain from the night before. The tiny drops of water glistened in the morning sunshine.

"Percival!" she called. "Percival!"

There was no answer. No response. The animal did not move. She climbed into the pen and ran to him, dropping onto her knees. She touched him on his damp side, on his wet head. There was no movement. No breath. No life.

"Percival!" she cried. "Percival!" she cried and cried.

Dave abandoned his plan for the morning and took charge, ringing the vet, taking the corpse to the practice to be examined. Emily followed him in a zombified state. Percival was dead. Tony and Alison had entrusted him to her, and she had let him die. He had not been in her care for even 24 hours, and she had let him die. And Dave did not care! All he cared about was being an 'action man', sorting out the problem of a dead sheep. He didn't say how sorry he was. He didn't put his arm around her to comfort her. She sat in the car crying, at the vet's crying, and at the kitchen table crying. She called Alison and then Julie to give them the bad news and cried with them on her phone.

"Poison," the vet said.

Poison? How was that possible? The vet asked them detailed questions. Was Percival well before he left Essex?

Had his journey been smooth? What else was in pen, and what grew around it? It was most likely, the vet decided, that Percival had been able to reach his head further into the bank at the back than anyone thought possible and had eaten something poisonous, probably fungus. An autopsy would show them for sure. It wasn't their fault. They couldn't have known. Emily felt drained. Flattened. Guilty.

There wasn't any lunch. The papers went unread. The DIY was left for another week. Back at home, the rims of Leo's eyes were as red as his mother's. Chris was relieved that the embarrassing pet was no more. At first, Emily thought that Dave's camp was somewhere between his sons', sandwiched between the sadness of accidental death and the practical relief of no longer being a sheep owner.

"Well, it's probably for the best, Em," Dave said. "It wasn't very sensible to have a sheep. They're not really pets. He'd have been nothing but a problem for us in the long run. Why don't you get a dog? I think we could manage a dog, couldn't we, boys?"

"You never wanted him, did you?" she cried.

"Want who, Emily? Who are you talking about?"

"Percival!" she shrieked.

"Now, Em, calm down. You've had a difficult day, and you know that's not true. I liked Percival just as much as anybody did."

"But you didn't love him."

"Of course not. Who could love a sheep?"

He looked at his watch and checked his jeans pocket for his car key, beginning to warm to the thought of a dog that they could all take for walks.

"Are you coming, Em?" he asked. "The film will start soon." He needed to rescue something from his plan for the day.

Emily didn't move from her seat at the kitchen table. She didn't look at Dave. She could hardly bear to look at him. His words made her sick. Fleetingly, she wondered if he knew fungi were poisonous for sheep and had deliberately allowed Percival to be poisoned 'accidentally' as he was the one of them that had read up on how to look after sheep, and it was him that had built the pen. Whatever the truth, it was clear to her that he couldn't see how much she loved Percival or how much she needed this unusual pet she'd first met in a painting. Did he understand her, even love her at all?

She could sense her sheep under the table nuzzling at her calves. It felt comforting to have him back with her again, and she put her hand down instinctively to tickle his curly head. She realised he was lifting his hoof and patting her lap to get her attention. "There's more to life than this," he seemed to be saying to her. "There's more to life than me."

"No, Dave," she said quietly.

She stood up and felt her little sheep push her from behind, encouraging her to keep going. "I don't want to go with you to the cinema. I loved that sheep."

Her sheep was prancing away from her down the hall

towards the front door. She picked up her handbag and followed.

"Where are you going?" Dave asked, caught out by the strength of his wife's unexplained intention.

"Out," she called back over her shoulder to her baffled husband and sons in the kitchen.

She opened the front door and followed her imaginary sheep into the glorious August evening sunshine. Things were going to change. She didn't know how exactly what she would do. But there was going to be a change, and she knew, at last, that she would be happier for it.

SMOKEY

SMOKEY

Nothing had gone right for Derek so far that day. He'd got himself into a muddle with his internet banking in the morning, transferring £820 - his contribution to the annual family cottage holiday on the Gower Peninsular - to the wrong son. Not disastrous, just irritating, and indicative of his mind not being on the job. He'd feign it as a memory lapse owing to general busyness and hope that no eyebrows would be raised. At lunchtime, he knocked a bottle of ketchup onto the kitchen floor when reaching too hastily for the oil in the cupboard next to the hob. It had smashed, splattering thick globules of tomato, slaughtered by shards of glass, across the counter, the floor, the cupboard doors.

He stood silently looking at the mess before taking his phone out of his pocket to check for the umpteenth time if she had sent a message. Of course, she hadn't. She said she would be busy in the morning and driving up from her sister's in Bristol in the afternoon.

"What a mess!" he murmured. Life or Ketchup?

If he wasn't incessantly checking the no-message phone, then his eyes were drawn to the clock; the aluminium-framed analogue mounted on the kitchen wall; the digital, with lime green numbers, on the oven front; the carriage clock with its hasty tick on the sitting room mantelpiece, all counting down the minutes, the seconds to 7 pm. The afternoon was stuck in treacle. He ought to buckle down and write his article, 'Theatrical pre-fabricated edifices at the Field of the Cloth of Gold' for *The Historian,* a magazine to which he contributed only occasionally now that he was retired. Instead, he was reading for pleasure. Well, actually, more like wrestling with text because he'd been told to. *Cloud Atlas*, recommended to him by his daughter-in-law, Alice. He felt he'd be bemused by the book even if he could concentrate.

"It's true many people find it hard work, Derek. But I can assure you it really is a very worthwhile read," she had declared in her slightly too fast, slightly too clipped, slightly too 'I know what's best for you' style. So, there he was, wrestling unsuccessfully with what he knew was, undoubtedly, a 'worthwhile' read and doing as his daughter-in-law suggested, as usual.

"Jane Austen's a worthwhile read." Derek dared to break the silence of his sitting room, not managing to get past page 28. "And suits my mood better," he added under his breath as he took a hobnob biscuit from the larder and poured himself a glass of cool sparkling water from the bottle chilling in his fridge. Guiltily, he lay aside Alice's diktat and headed with *Pride and Prejudice* to the rose-bedecked arbour in his garden, where, in the June afternoon sunshine, he sat in comfort, reading familiar pages with familiar phrases, creating a talisman to force his nervousness about the evening ahead of him, to the basement of his brain.

At 5.58 pm, he left his sunny spot and went upstairs. He hadn't shaved that morning so that he could perform that getting-ready ritual this evening and be clean and fresh for dinner. Maybe that had been the wrong decision? Maybe even that slight change of routine had added to his distraction? His cheeks felt itchy, rough, uncomfortable. He wet shaved carefully, running the razor lightly over his ageing skin and then rummaged at the back of the bathroom cabinet, searching for some cologne or aftershave which might still be lurking and wearable.

When he had met Jenny, she had smelt of lilac - glorious, blousy, beautiful lilac. Was it a coincidence that it was May and the lilac was in bloom, he had wondered? She seemed to be lilac personified, with her silver-blonde hair, purply eyes, soft rose blush and lips. She had wafted into the room where he was the guest speaker, like a breath of lilac-scented air, mauve dress swishing, pink beads at her throat. She had sat in the front row. Derek could hardly concentrate. The title had been 'Renaissance Queens of France,' but instead of Catherine de Medici and Diane de Poitiers, he could only think about the lilac lady in the front row. When she had raised her hand to ask a question, he had felt that his answer had been an embarrassing tongue-tied drivel.

At the end of the session, as he was packing away his PowerPoint presentation, the lilac lady approached him with a cup of tea balanced precariously on a saucer.

"Thank you for a most interesting talk. Would you like a cup of tea?" she smiled like a fresh May day, offering him the tea, which he took with a nervous nod.

"I don't normally come to these history society lectures, but I'm new to the area. I've moved to be near my daughter. She's expecting twins in the autumn. I've been meaning to move closer for years, but I've got no excuse not to now," she said.

The lilac lady sang her words in a lyric south Wales melody, offering more details of her life in a few phrases than

Derek felt he'd be able to convey about his own in a novel.

"I'm sure she'll be grateful," was all he could think to say as he inhaled her lilac fragrance and found his knees wobbling.

"Oh, you must be tired after your talk."

She had noticed his slight tremor and put it down to the fatigue of the evening. She did not have the slightest inkling that her presence, her fragrance, had caused it.

"Let's sit down," she said. And she drew him to the front row seats, where she had sat earlier.

She chatted freely about the court of François the First of France and her own family, and questioned him on his with such an easy, warm manner that before he knew it, he too was mixing stories of the French King and the glamour-boy young Henry VIII with those of his grown-up sons and their children. After a while, he became vaguely aware that the sound of other conversations in the hall had quietened as the society members drifted home and that the musical clinking of china cups and saucers, which had come from the hall's kitchenette, had ceased now that all had been washed up and put away. Jenny seemed in no hurry to bring her comments on his talk or her questions about his family or his life in the town to a close, and neither, he realised, was he. They were still talking as, in slight embarrassment that they were the only two left in the hall, they helped Janet Cleary, the chair of the History Society and organiser-in-chief, stack the chairs and lock up.

"Well, goodnight. It was nice to meet you, Derek," Jenny

sang in the fading light as they parted. She seemed to float to her car. In the dusk, she left behind a lingering smell of lilac and Derek, slightly bemused, wondering what had just happened.

Janet Cleary proved then to be a good friend. He had known her for a long time. She had been a friend of Wendy's first. He couldn't remember how Wendy and Janet had met. Perhaps at their mother and toddler group, or maybe it was sharing lifts to junior school football matches around the county. A long time ago, whatever the exact number of years. Janet had been more than a friend, she had been a good friend, the best. She had joined the rota to take Wendy to the chemo treatments as he couldn't manage them all and his work commitments at the university. She had helped out around the house. He had been astonished one day when he came in from grocery shopping to find her changing the sheets on Wendy's bed. He hadn't realised that was something else he ought to have been doing. Janet picked up the pieces. And she continued to pick up the pieces with casseroles and kindness when it was obvious that no chemotherapy, radiotherapy, drugs, positive thinking and prayers were going to keep Wendy with them any longer.

"Just a little lunch party for my birthday. You will come, won't you, Derek?" Janet cooed into the phone a week after the History Society meeting. "There will be quite a few people you know."

And there were, including the lilac lady.

"Derek, this is Jenny. You met at the History Society," Janet said lightly, handing them each a glass of birthday prosecco before breezing off and leaving them to it.

Derek was momentarily tongue-tied and stooped forward slightly as he was prone to do when unsure of himself. She was so pretty. Her manner was so relaxed. He wanted to put his arms wide around her, draw her to himself, melt into her fragrance and flesh, to breathe her in as lilac blossom.

Away from the firm footing of his beloved history, Derek launched into the obvious,

"Um, so you come from Wales?"

"Abergavenny. I come from Abergavenny," she said softly, comfortingly. "Do you know it?"

Funny how they had not touched on it before, so tied up they had been in French history and the moment of meeting in the fading light of the well-used and slightly tired church hall.

"Not too well," he replied, wishing it was otherwise. "But we go to Tenby and the Gower Peninsula. We've been going every year since the boys were small. Now we all go together with the grandchildren. I think I told you about them the other evening. There's six of them - two boys and four girls, funny as we just had two lads…"

He'd gone on a bit, he had known. And he had ended up talking far too much about Wendy, about how she had loved Wales, what great times they had had there, how she had only met two of the six grandchildren and what a sadness that was. Jenny was just as lilac as she had been at the History Society lecture, but later that evening, he was convinced that he must have given her the wrong impression. Why had he spoken so much about Wendy when he wanted to talk about Wales to Jenny - who, after all, was Welsh? Why had he dwelt so much on life with his dead wife, when he wanted to ask this new lady about hers?

Derek lingered when all the other guests had left to help his friends tidy up - running the vacuum cleaner around while Philip restored furniture to its day to day position and Janet loaded the dishwasher. When all was done, the three collapsed into the living room easy-chairs, sinking into the assorted Laura Ashley cushions in a pleasant state of post-party fatigue and sipping well-earned cups of decaf coffee.

"Jenny's very nice, don't you think?" Janet commented more than asked. "And she seemed to get on with everyone."

"Quite brave to up and move like that at her age," Philip offered.

"What are you talking about 'at her age?'" Janet bristled. "She's got to be younger than me. Anyway, she said her sister's in Bristol, and she has one daughter in London, not showing any signs of settling down - working all hours for a barristers' chambers, and another daughter here who needs her."

"What happened to her husband?" Derek asked quietly, almost nonchalantly, almost as if not caring.

"Jenny told me they split up years ago," Janet explained. "He's remarried and settled in Penzance, or was it Truro? Cornwall anyway."

"Interesting," Derek remarked casually, sitting back,

folding his arms, leaving his body language to end the conversation.

But Janet was going to have none of that!

"You know, Derek, it's ok to find other women attractive and to ask them out."

Derek nearly fell out of his comfortable armchair, so thrown was he by Janet's remark.

"Anyone can see you like her," Janet continued her offensive. "The pair of you were just fizzing at the History Society. Why do you think I invited her to my birthday?"

"Janet, please!" Derek begged.

"Is it not because you are kind and wanted to help her settle into the area?" Philip piped up, his brown eyes sparkling with merriment. He loved it when Janet was in this kind of mood.

"Philip, don't tease!" Janet said crossly. "Seriously, Derek, Wendy died five years ago now. If you meet someone you like, you must make an effort."

Derek looked like he was going to cry, but Janet pursued, nevertheless.

"Why don't you ask her out?"

"I can't do that. I don't know how to. It's been too long."

"I think you will find that people still go on dates to restaurants and cinemas."

"Cafés too," Philip added.

"… lectures, garden centres, art galleries. Just suggest somewhere you both might like to spend some time together and get to know each other better," Janet said.

Derek put his hands to his head and groaned. He looked like he was heading for an aeroplane crash position.

"I don't remember how Wendy and I started going out - it just seemed to happen. We were terribly young."

"She probably told you to do it."

"Philip! That's not helpful."

But true, both the men thought. Derek did seem to have a curious ability to be surrounded by women who told him what to do. That was easier than making a decision, especially one that impacted day-to-day life or the well-being of the people around you. The thought of Jenny filled his mind. He did want to see her again. Very much.

"Do you think she likes me, Janet, honestly? Don't you think I'm too old for this?" Derek looked up at Janet from his aeroplane crash position, eyes full of hope yet fearful.

"For goodness' sake, Derek, you've only just turned 70. Of course, you're not too old. I'll ask her if I can give you her number, and then you can take it from there. Message her if you feel talking's too much."

Panicked, Derek looked to Philip for reassurance, confirmation, a let-out.

"She did seem very nice, and I think you could probably get through a dinner with her," Philip responded.

Poor Derek didn't have the confidence to call Jenny outright, so he messaged. She had spoken very highly of a historical novel that she had read recently. Could she remind him of the author and the title as he would like to read it? Of course, she could, but better than that, she would lend it to him. They could meet, and she could give it to him. When? Dinner, perhaps on Wednesday night? Where? A new Thai restaurant in town had just opened (Please, God let her like Thai) - an opportunity for them both to try a new place. (Maybe that was a mistake, maybe he should have suggested a restaurant that he had been to before and that he knew would be good and where he would feel comfortable?)

The messages on their phones pinged back and forth as they made their arrangements, his in a green speech bubble and hers in a white. Curious conversation, filled with the ability to read the whole exchange again and again, yet the inability to hear the tone, the expression, the nerves, the warmth. How different to his first conversations with Wendy, where he had collected coins and stuffed them into the slot in the phone box, freezing in the winter chill, huddling over the phone, and speaking into the receiver in an almost whisper so that the person waiting for their turn in the red booth after him could not hear.

"See you Tuesday!"

"See you Tuesday!" They had laugh-shouted as his pile of coins ran out, the end-of-time beeps sounded, and the call was cut. Silence. Happy silence. He would leave the phone box with a smile, holding the door open for the next caller, sensibly wrapped in coat, gloves, scarf and bobble hat, who would either already have their coin in their mitted hand or would be fumbling in their pocket to find it.

Now Derek stood in his bedroom at 6.17 pm, having survived the day so far. He paused in front of the long mirror which hung from the wall on Wendy's side of the room. What had Jenny seen him in? What did he see in himself? His hair was still a good colour, even if it was mousey, and although thinning, it still covered his head. It was true he was weightier than he had been as a young man, but he could not be described as portly. He did stoop a bit, he knew. Alice was always telling him to stand up tall. He pushed his head forward and up, made his shoulders square, and looked at his new reflection. He didn't seem to be any more himself than he was before. So he let his posture sink to its habitual place with a sigh. 6.20 pm. He had better get ready.

He had decided what to wear this evening at least three days ago. He reached into his wardrobe and pulled out a pale grey silk shirt, the exact shade of his eyes. It was comfortable, and it made him feel handsome. He chose a pink tie and dark grey trousers to go with it. The shirt was double-cuffed, so he took a pair of sterling silver cufflinks in the shape of eagles that he had bought for Kevin and Alice's wedding from a small Indian box, a souvenir from a special holiday before Wendy got sick. Would it be too warm for a blazer being June? He wasn't sure. Perhaps not the tie? Maybe that was too formal? He took it off. 6.26 pm, and he was ready.

What would she wear, he wondered? He liked the lilac floral dress of the History Society. What would they talk about? What topics other than children, Wales or Renaissance history might they discuss? Books, perhaps? At least he could comment on *Cloud Atlas* and *Pride and Prejudice*.

Or films, maybe? The recent adaptation of *Emma* was rather good and filmed locally. Would she still like him after dinner? What would happen after dinner? Should he pay the whole bill, or would that be insulting? Would she let him kiss her? Please God, let her let him kiss her. If she did, should he kiss her on the cheek or the lips? The thoughts spun round and round like a carousel in his head as he stood looking at his reflection. The grey shirt did bring out his grey eyes.

He had decided that he wanted to take Jenny out for dinner. Philip and Janet's suggestions of a date at a garden centre or a café had sounded too casual. Jenny was special. A date should be special, even if it is terrifying. The new Thai restaurant in the town centre, he agreed with himself, was perfect for Jenny. The walls were covered in a beautiful floral wallpaper with petal swirls of pink, lilac, and pale lemon, set among spring green leaves. A bower of indistinct, interior-designed flowers bringing remembrance of exotic holidays in a place other than here. He arrived at the restaurant first and, standing slightly to the side of entrance, spiralled his elbow away from his body so that his wristwatch peeked at him from below his grey shirt. It was 6:58, nearly 7 pm. He would have preferred to have been even earlier, to be on the safe side.

When Jenny arrived she was all roses, wearing a blush floribunda print dress and a pretty dark pink cardigan softened with a frill at the sleeve and the collar. She leaned into him to greet him with a short friendly kiss on the cheek, and as she did, he caught the smell of freshly applied rose perfume. When they said goodbye, she lingered on her parting kiss. Still cheek to cheek, but now with his hand on her arm, Derek inhaled the fading aroma of roses, Jenny, and a happy evening.

"Well, how did you get on?" Janet asked the following day, with undisguised curiosity.

He had only answered the phone because she had rung on the landline. If she had called his mobile, her name 'Janet' would have flashed up with the ringing tone, and he would have ignored the call, letting her leave a voicemail message, which he could also ignore. There was no such facility on the landline making it impossible to know who was calling. It could be one of those annoying recorded messages, or it could be urgent business, which is why he had answered it, which is why Janet had called it.

"Oh, hello, Janet," he replied, not answering her question.

"Derek!" she exclaimed. "Don't hold me in suspense. How did it go with Jenny?"

He twisted the phone cord in his hand and looked out of the window. He felt rooted to his spot. He was caught in Janet's aural gaze.

"Of course, I can always ask Jenny," she continued, somewhat slyly.

"No, don't do that!"

"Well?"

He knew that she had his best interests at heart, but he didn't like the manipulation. He stood in silence, remembering the evening.

"It went fine," he answered. And then repeated in disbelief, "It went fine!"

"And are you going to see each other again?" Janet asked.

"Ye-es," he answered, drawing the vowel through a giggle of astonishment and relief.

"Oh, that's great, Derek! Terrific! Go on, tell me more. Where? When?" She questioned urgently, in a girlish squeal. She sounded like an excited teenager complicit in a best friend's love life.

"On Friday. She's invited me to supper at her house."

"Alone?"

"I think so. She didn't mention anyone else." A cloud passed over his face. He had assumed it would be just the two of them. He hoped it would be.

"Well, it doesn't matter whether it's just you or not. It's great that you are seeing each other again so soon."

****

Alice was disappointed that he couldn't have fish and chips with the grandchildren on Friday. Disappointed or irritated that she would have to find an official babysitter for once. It wasn't as if he'd been invited to Kevin and Alice's. Yes, he did go there most Friday evenings when his son's family weren't doing something together; yes, Alice and Kevin often used it as an opportunity to go out alone. This Friday, it was him doing something else. It was him going out. How daring! He was daring to do something that Alice hadn't told him to do. He was daring to go to supper at Jenny's house.

Tonight was his second date with Jenny and their fourth time meeting. Derek still felt nervous. He still watched the clock and counted down the minutes until the evening. He tried gardening to quell his anxiety. The gentle rhythm of weeding and deadheading countered the worries that prowled like a tiger around his mind, somewhat better than admin and reading had done a few days before. He felt sure now that Jenny liked him. She messaged him several times a day. The more they talked, the more they discovered shared interests. She wasn't keen on the theatre and preferred the cinema, like him. She loved Southern Europe - France, Italy, Spain, Portugal - as he did, but had not explored the northern countries; neither had he. She was excited at the prospect of becoming a grandmother very soon. The joy of being a grandparent was something they would share, and she looked forward to it.

He liked to listen to her talk. Her lyrical accent was a song that held him entranced. When she spoke about the subjects which interested her, her face danced. To Derek, she was a beautiful film star from the golden age of Hollywood, whom the camera held in a loving close-up. He could watch her all day. He could gaze at her soft, feminine face for eternity. God, he wanted to kiss her. So much he wanted to kiss her. Her lips, her cheeks, her brow, her face, her neck. Should he kiss her tonight? Would she let him kiss her tonight? Not just a peck on the cheek. He wanted more than that. Much more.

Jenny lived as close to the centre of the town as he did but in the other direction. The spell of fine summer evenings was as yet unbroken, and as her house was probably no more than a mile away, Derek walked there. He passed the church hall where they had met not so very long ago. He passed the new Thai, where a new set of diners were enjoying a pleasant evening out. He passed the fountain, the centrepiece of the town's grass boulevard landscape, and paused for a few seconds to watch the crystal drops rise into the air and plunge into its aqua pool. Here, he left the pavement to walk on the grass. His steps hugged the deep flowerbed borders filled with roses and lavender, and his thoughts were full of Jenny. At the end of the boulevard, he continued over the white, art-deco bridge which spanned the disused railway, now a leisure path through the woods. The elegant, old-fashioned lamps moulded into the statue pillars made the bridge feel like a theatrical gateway to a new scene of a play.

Her house was a little 1920s cottage, not far from the bridge, in a quiet cul-de-sac, so typical of the town. Derek paused at the end of the road and checked his watch - 7.29 pm. He had timed the walk well. He waited for the digits to change to 7:30, then approached her house, number 3, and rang the bell.

"Hello," she sang-welcomed him when she opened the door, eyes, mouth, cheeks, throat and silver hair all smiling at him. "You found your way ok?"

"Yes, I know the road," he replied. "I brought you this," he said, handing her a sweet pea patterned bottle bag. "And these are from my garden. I hope you like them," he added, shyly presenting her with a posy.

She took the bottle bag from him, and peeping in, she

saw it contained a bottle of white wine. She admired the posy of yellow roses and white daisies. It was an unusual and slightly rustic combination. It could not have come from a florist and was all the better for that, she thought, understanding the sincerity in the bunch and the trouble it had taken.

"Thank you. They're lovely." She murmured as she lowered her nose into the roses and daisies. Pollen dust tickled her nostrils, and she sneezed.

"Excuse me!"

"Bless you."

They laughed, both slightly nervous.

"Oh, dear. I get a touch of hay fever from time to time."

"That's a pity," he said, worried that he had brought her an unwelcome gift.

"It's no matter. I love the flowers. Thank you so much. Come and sit down while I put them in a vase. Can I get you a drink? What would you like? Sherry? Wine? Red or white? Whiskey?"

"What are you having?"

"A gin and tonic."

"I'd like that then, please."

She bustled into the kitchen with her bottle and flower gifts, showing him into the sitting room on her way. It was at the front of the house, with a bay window overlooking her well-kept front garden and with a view of the house on the opposite side of the cul-de-sac. There was a piano in the corner of the room used as a shelf for photographs of her daughters: babies sitting and crawling, little girls in checked school uniform dresses, and teenagers in holiday snaps on beaches and on boats. Now, adult, there were portraits of graduates in black gowns and mortar boards and a white bride, her arms around her sister, a mint-green bridesmaid. At the front of the display, was space for new photos of new babies.

A coffee table stood on a cream and blue mat in the middle of the room. Lying on top of it, was a copy of *History Today* and a novel with a bookmark poking out, marking the page she had reached before laying it to one side. By the piano, a duck-egg armchair invited guests to nestle into plumped-up velvet cushions of dark claret. Along the wall opposite the window, beneath a rather attractive original painting of a woodland landscape, a duck-egg sofa, matching the armchair, was festooned with cushions of claret velvet and floral print, placed welcomingly side by side. And to his right, almost behind the open door, was another armchair and, on it, a cat.

Oh my God. She has a cat!

If Derek had been feline, all his hair would have stood up on end in horror and dismay.

"A cat!" he moaned.

It was a large, sleek cat, the colour of polished ebony. It lay nonchalantly on a beige blanket - the cat's blanket on the cat's chair. The cat raised its head at Derek and stared at him with its amber eyes.

"Miaow," it said, greeting the stranger who had come into the room. The cat was too self-assured to be bothered by the newcomer, but it was interested in him.

Derek did not reply. Should he stay in the room or leave quickly and go to the kitchen? What if he went to the garden before the worst happened, and suggested to his hostess that they have their drink and meal outside in the evening sun?

"Miaow," the cat mewed again.

"I'm just coming," he heard Jenny call from the kitchen.

The air in Derek's lungs began to feel thick. What should he do? What could he do? he panicked.

Jenny returned carrying a tray with two glasses of gin and tonic with ice and lemon and the posy of flowers he had given her, now in a ceramic vase that was cobalt blue at its base fading to palest turquoise at its rim. She placed the tray on the coffee table next to the magazine and the book.

"Thank you so much for the lovely flowers," she said again. "Please sit down, Derek." As she spoke, she indicated a place on the sofa and handed him one of the glasses of gin and tonic. He hesitated, unwilling to sit.

"Miaow," the cat mewed, seeking its owner's attention. And this time, it stood up on the chair and stretched its legs and arms. It arched its back and then jumped down onto the floor, landing with a soft thud-thud on the carpet.

"I see you've met Smokey," she said.

She bent down, and with gin and tonic in one hand, she tickle-caressed Smokey's jaw and neck with the other.

"Smokey, this is Derek," she introduced.

"Miaow."

What was he meant to say? Derek coughed the phlegm in his throat away.

"Hello, Smokey," he said weakly.

Jenny stood up and Smokey brushed his body against her legs, first one way and then the other.

"Cheers," she said, raising her glass to Derek's. The glasses chinked pleasantly together.

They both sat down on the sofa.

Smokey investigated the man in the room. In his 'This is my house, and I'm doing you a favour to let you in it' manner. He smelt the toes of Derek's shoes and then sniffed around to his ankles. His whiskers touched Derek's shins, feeling the man, smelling him out. Derek stayed perfectly still. If he didn't move, the creature might lose interest and disappear. He held his drink tight in one hand and gripped his knee in the other.

Poor Derek, Jenny thought. *He's still so nervous, but he needn't be.*

"Smokey likes you," she said. "Don't you, Smokey?" Pets and children. Always such an icebreaker.

Receiving no attention from Derek, Smokey gave up and jumped onto Jenny's lap. She took him as a baby into her arms, his head nestled in the crook of her elbow, their faces almost touching, woman and cat almost kissing.

"Oh my Smokey-pokey, you funny furry bundle," she cooed.

The cat purred in response - a deep, satisfying, velvet rumble.

"I do love you, my Smokey-pokey," she said. "My good boy. My good Smokey."

For an instant, Jenny hardly seemed aware that Derek was in the room.

She rocked her cat and cooed her love. Smokey purred and humoured her in the embrace. Fine feline hairs, covered with dust from his skin and pollen from the garden, drifted into the sitting-room air as Jenny cuddled her cat. Derek could see delicate strands of fluff and fine spots of dust caught in the golden evening light which streamed through the bay window. His chest tightened. His nostrils itched.

"Achoo!" He sneezed.

"Bless you," Jenny said, pulled from her reverie by the noise and almost surprised to see her guest in the room.

"Achoo!"

"Oh dear, it must be the flowers!"

Smokey wriggled and jumped down from her arms.

Derek searched through his pockets for a handkerchief. There wasn't one. He gave up, wondering if he could excuse himself and go to the bathroom for some toilet tissue.

"Shall I take the flowers out?" she asked.

"No, it's fine," he wheezed, embarrassed that his nose was beginning to run.

"Would you like a tissue?" she asked, putting Smokey down on the carpet at their feet and moving over to a bookcase near Smokey's chair where there was a cube box of Kleenex.

He hadn't noticed the bookcase when he entered. It was almost as full of photos as it was of books. Unlike the images on the piano, these photos were all of a cat, of Smokey. Smokey in the garden, Smokey on a chair, Smokey in Jenny's arms, Smokey in her bed. Each one in a frame, like those of her daughters.

She handed him the tissues, and pulling one out from its cardboard nest, he blew his nose as quietly and as unremarkably as he could.

"Are you alright, Derek?" she asked with a face full of concern.

"Yes, thank you. Nothing that a good gin and tonic can't fix." He laughed the sneezing off and raised his glass in another toast before taking several good, deep sips.

She joined him.

Not to be left out, Smokey jumped up onto the sofa and into the space between them, turning around twice in a circle before settling down. More cat hair flew up as he did so. Derek held his breath and shrank his back into his sofa corner seat, trying to avoid the contamination.

"Good boy, Smokey," Jenny said, stroking him.

They sat in silence. The loud purr from Smokey's throat was the only sound. Derek, concentrating on breathing a little bit in, a little bit out, could not speak, and Jenny suddenly could think of nothing to say. She finished her gin, and seeing that Derek's glass was also empty, asked if he would like some more. He nodded, and she took their glasses out to the kitchen to pour them both another.

Why, in God's name, did she have to have a cat? He thought ruefully as a wave of sadness washed over him, numbing him as if it were gin.

He couldn't be jealous of Smokey, could he? Jenny thought to herself as she poured out the gin and took a good gulp from her glass before topping it up. *This won't work if he's jealous of Smokey.*

A little light-headed from her gin and tonic, she took a packet of Bombay mix from the larder, and poured the spicy assortment into a little dish she had bought in Tenby years ago. Returning to the sitting room with the gin and the snack, she found Derek pressed against the end of the sofa with Smokey next to him. Smokey had given Derek up in disgust and was ignoring the man as much as the man was ignoring the cat. To prove his point, Smokey was now washing, licking his back and breast without a care.

Maybe he doesn't like cats? Jenny thought. *That's not going to work, either.*

She shut the door to the hall before handing Derek the second gin and tonic and offering him some Bombay Mix.

He knew he should say something - he had to rescue the

evening, somehow.

"Have you had Smokey long?" he asked her, trying his best to disguise the wheeze that accompanied his out-breath. Then he quickly blew his nose before another sneeze grabbed him.

So he does like cats! She smiled as she replied,

"No, not really. Not long for a cat. He's six. He could live well into his 'teens."

She stroked his black-as-soot back as she spoke and Smokey stopped washing to look up at her, offering his face and neck for another tender caress.

"How did he cope with your move?"

"Very well. He's quite an explorer. That's because he's a male cat. Although I did have him neutered - I couldn't bear the thought of him fathering unwanted litters of kittens." she added apologetically. Derek felt embarrassed. It was more detail than he wanted to know when he had asked the question.

"He still goes out on great long excursions around the neighbourhood. If I'd moved when he was a kitten or a young cat, I'd have been worried he wouldn't have found his way home. But he's got more sense now he's a grown-up puss. Haven't you Smokey-pokey?" she rubbed his head and throat as she spoke, and he looked up at her with what appeared to Derek to be adoring eyes.

"He means so much to me," she said softly. "I can get quite lonely, living by myself. When he goes out, he always comes home. That can't be said for everyone you love," she added in a tone so low and so much to herself that it hardly reached Derek's ears.

He was trying to listen to her, but a blasted speck of cat hair had drifted into his left eye. He had made the mistake of rubbing it as she was talking, and now hot tears that had no hope of quenching the itch beneath the skin at the edge of the eye were streaming down his face. His right eye broke out in sympathy. Tears rolled from both, as lava erupts from a volcano, providing no relief, only more scorching irritation.

Jenny looked up at him. She was surprised to see him crying. Her comments about her cat must have moved him. He was such a kind and thoughtful, caring man. She smiled at him gratefully and offered him more Bombay Mix.

As the bowl passed over his head, Smokey reached up to sniff it. Food, but not to his taste. He stood up, stretched, jumped down from the sofa and sidled up the shut door, where he mewed loudly to be let out.

"You want your dinner, don't you, Smokey?" She said to the cat, then turning to Derek, she added, "He won't bother us now. He'll eat what I gave him earlier, and then he will go out into the garden. The days are so long now that he won't think to come back into the house until well past midnight. Will you, Smokey? What do you find out there, even in a town? Mice? Shrews?"

He miaowed again. What was taking her so long to let him out? She finished her gin and tonic and opened the door to the hall. Smokey shot past her feet, fast on his paws.

Thank God! Derek thought in relief and finished his drink.

****

Poor Derek slept fitfully. As he had in his darkest days, he turned to his good friend, Janet, calling her on her mobile at breakfast time.

"Derek? How did it go?"

"Awfully. Oh, Janet, it was terrible," he groaned.

"What happened?" An absolute disaster must have occurred for Derek to call her. Everything seemed to be going so well for her friend. Jenny and Derek seemed to be so suitable for each other.

"Derek?" she said softly, encouraging his confidence. "What happened?"

"She's got a cat!" he burst out.

"She's got a cat?" Janet repeated, groping in the dark to understand the problem.

"I'm allergic to cats," Derek said angrily. Angry at himself. Angry at the cat. "I'm badly allergic to cats."

"Oh yes, of course. I'm sorry, Derek, I forgot."

"It was terrible. I couldn't breathe, my eyes were stinging, my nose was running, I was sneezing all over the place."

"Couldn't you have taken an antihistamine?"

"I didn't have any. And anyway, antihistamine doesn't

work very well for me."

"Well, that must have been rather uncomfortable, but surely Jenny understands."

"I didn't tell her."

"You didn't tell her?"

"No. I just sat there streaming and feeling terrible."

"Why didn't you tell her what was wrong, Derek?"

"Because she loves the cat."

"Owners of cats usually do love them, Derek."

"No, Janet, Jenny really loves this cat. She held it like a baby. She's got a whole bookcase with shelves filled with photos of him. I couldn't tell her that her cat was making me sick and ask her to put it out. She might as well have put me out!"

Even when Smokey had left the house for the garden, Derek had still felt unwell. He wheezed his way through what would have been a delicious supper and left at 9.15 pm, much earlier than he would have liked, excusing himself with a bit of a cold. Jenny took his hand on his departure and shook it goodbye. She didn't kiss him. He felt miserable every step home, but at least the fresh air cleared his lungs. He, too, knew what it felt like to return to a lonely, empty home.

"You'll have to tell her you're allergic to her cat," Janet said, resuming her bossy tone.

"I can't," Derek replied, feeling very sorry for himself.

Now Janet was cross. How could her friend let romance fall at the first hurdle? Was it such a problem to be allergic to the cat of the woman you would like to have as a girlfriend, a prospective partner even? She took a deep breath and was about to launch into the usual cajoling tirade she reserved especially for Derek when he said quietly, "Do you think you could tell her, Janet? Could you tell Jenny that I'm allergic to her cat?" He sounded so small, like a sad child. Janet softened, and sighed. She just wanted him to be happy. The sweet man deserved to be happy.

"Yes, Derek. I'll tell her," she promised, ending the call with a goodbye.

"Bloody hell, Derek!" Janet swore-muttered as she put the phone into her handbag on the kitchen chair.

Philip was sitting at the table, eating his breakfast as quietly as he could.

"You heard all that?" she questioned grimly.

He nodded.

"The things I do for that friend of ours," she complained.

"Yes, but you love it," her husband replied cheekily.

"I suppose I do," she relented. "But, honestly, Philip, to mediate in a cat allergy bust-up is almost the limit."

"You'll do it wonderfully," he assured her and kissed her on her cheek before putting his empty breakfast bowl and spoon into the dishwasher.

****

Janet needn't have worried about her assignment, because she never had the opportunity to fulfil it. On Saturday, the day after the disastrous supper date, Derek and Jenny had exchanged thank-you pleasantries on their phones. On Sunday, he had messaged her, and she had not replied. On Monday, there was no exchange between them at all. He picked his phone up again and again throughout the day to check that he had not missed an alert, but she had not contacted him, and he did not like to send messages where they were not wanted. He popped into Kevin and Alice's at teatime. At least he knew he'd be appreciated there at the witching hour of bathtime-bedtime and could sit down with them both with a large glass of wine once their brood was all asleep. They knew nothing about Jenny, so there would be no questions. No thoughts of his lilac lady, his garden rose love. Two more days passed. Two more long, no-message days. Derek found refuge in his study, intending to research a new article, 'Mary Queen of Scots: The Child Bride in France'. But the pages of his books meant nothing to him, and his internet searches took him around in circles. Seconds disappeared to minutes, to hours, and by the afternoon, the article was no further advanced than its title. Then on Thursday, his phone pinged. A sound that could have been missed if Derek hadn't been hoping for it. He read her message and immediately pressed the return call button. Smokey! It was Smokey! Her beloved cat had gone missing.

"Jenny, are you alright?" he stuttered into his phone. "I'm so sorry. Yes, of course, I'll come round. I'll bring Janet. She'll know what to do."

He looked at his watch: 4.34 pm. Philip would be at work, but Janet would be free.

****

He didn't need to ring the doorbell. Jenny had seen them coming from where she was waiting in the bay sitting room window, and she opened the door before he was even on the doorstep.

"I've looked everywhere for him," she cried out.

Her anxiety was too great for a standard greeting of hello. Derek could see that she had been crying. The rims of her eyes were red, and her mascara had run to form streaks of grey on her cheekbones.

"Well, we're here now to help you look everywhere again," he said gently.

Janet, at his shoulder, pushed past him.

"It'll be alright, Jenny." She took charge. "When did he disappear, and where have you looked?"

"It's been three days now. He's never been gone this long. He ate his dinner on Monday night and then went out, and I haven't seen him since. Something must have happened to him. He'd come home otherwise. I know he would." Her shoulders shook as she spoke, her eyes brimming with tears.

Janet put her arms around the weeping woman. Derek wished he could. He wanted to hug Jenny and feel her nestle into him as he made everything alright for her.

"Can I look in your garden - in your shed?" Derek said, hitting on something to do, which could be helpful, and outside away from cat hair and cat dust.

"Yes, of course, but he won't be there. I've checked already. The key's by the back door on a nail."

Derek went through the house to the kitchen and, finding the key, took the path to the shed. Cats, he knew, were always getting stuck in sheds. The most likely place would be in her own. He remembered how James, his youngest, had gone missing when he was about three years old. The family had searched in panic for what seemed like hours but was probably only twenty minutes. He had checked the shed himself, but there had been no sign of little James within. A while later, when all the cupboards and wardrobes had been searched, and every bed looked under, and neighbours, having checked their premises, were now helping Wendy comb the road, Derek thought to check the shed again - and there he had found little James fast asleep, curled up inside an upturned cardboard box.

He looked carefully through all the boxes and behind all the garden equipment in Jenny's shed, but there was no sign of Smokey. Disheartened, he returned to the house where Janet had a pot of tea brewing for them all and was busy making a list of different places to search.

"Have you called the local vets?" Janet asked.

"Yes. He's chipped. The vet would call me if someone's found him and called them."

"That would be the same for the Cats Protection

League," Janet said. "But my friend is a volunteer at the local branch. I'll call her and ask her to put a message out on Facebook."

"Thank you," Jenny said. "I'm so glad you're here to help."

Derek felt a twinge of jealousy. He was helping too. He was the one whom Jenny had called. It was just that Janet was taking charge.

"Smokey's not in the shed," he said.

"I knew he wouldn't be."

"I could make a 'missing cat' poster on the computer and put it up," Derek suggested brightly.

"That's a great idea, Derek," Janet replied before Jenny could answer for herself.

"That's if you'd like me to, Jenny?" he asked hesitantly, yet hopefully.

Jenny smiled her thanks at him. Derek felt that a little ray of sunshine had come into the room.

"I wouldn't know how to make a poster," she said. "Thank you, Derek. Thank you very much."

"Could I use your computer, Jenny? I could do it now, and then we could put it up on the lampposts and trees as we search. Do you have a photo of him I can use?"

He knew she had photographs of Smokey - lots.

The computer was in the spare bedroom upstairs, and

Derek was relieved that it did not seem to be a room in which Smokey had spent much time. With little cat hair in the air, he would be alright, for a while at least. Downstairs they could hear Janet on the phone with her friend at the Cats Protection League. Jenny logged on and found Derek a recent photo of her beloved cat. It was a close-up of him sitting, his paws curled in and tucked under his body, his coat soft and gleaming. Smokey had deigned to look into the camera long enough with his amber eyes for an elegant portrait snap to have been taken. It was not difficult for Derek to assemble a missing cat poster. It was hardly a work of art, but it would do the job.

Armed with Janet's battle plan and Derek's posters, the three friends rang the doorbells of all the houses in the pretty cul de sac and the surrounding streets. Where neighbours were in, they introduced themselves and explained that Smokey was missing - could they please look in their sheds, their garages, keep their eyes out for him? Where there was no reply, they posted one of Derek's 'missing cat' posters through the door. They went as far as they thought he might roam, further even.

No one had seen Smokey.

Tired and depressed, they returned to Jenny's cottage, each thinking the worst but clinging to the possibility that he would be found.

"Perhaps he's strayed too far and got himself lost. Someone will find him."

"If someone has, they could think they're being kind by feeding a stray. He might stay where there's food on offer."

"He wouldn't do that!"

"But he might."

"Yes, I guess he might."

"He's not the sort of cat that would be stolen, is he?"

"He's handsome, but he's not a special breed. No one would do that."

"He wouldn't jump in a car and be driven away by accident and then jump out when the car stops and not know how to get home, would he?"

Clutching at straws, they could not admit that poor Smokey could be dead.

As nothing more could be done that day, Janet and Derek left. Janet gave Jenny a supportive hug on her way out. Derek also wanted to, but he hung back with the same embarrassment that he had felt on arrival.

"Smokey will turn up. I'm sure of it," he said, wanting to stress again before he left that he understood how much her cat meant to her and how sorry he was for their disastrous date.

She looked sadly at him and answered with a sigh,

"I hope you're right."

And then, to his surprise and pleasure, she leant forward and kissed him goodbye on the cheek, saying, "Thank you, Derek. I'm grateful for everything you're doing to help me find my cat."

She shut the door behind her friends and felt overwhelmed by loneliness in her cat-less house. Everywhere she looked reminded her of Smokey. She didn't feel like being brave. She didn't feel like being her usual sunny self. So she went to his chair in the sitting room, wrapped herself in his blanket, and then picked up each framed photo of her beloved puss in turn, remembering each occasion that the cat had been snapped. *Smokey, please come home*, she thought to herself again and again as the evening faded into night.

Derek did what he could to cheer Jenny up. He took her for coffee in town, lunch at the garden centre, and a film at the cinema. She cooked him dinner, and in a clean, cat-less house, he didn't sneeze or wheeze.

Without mentioning it to her, he took down all the missing cat posters they had put up on the afternoon of their search. It had rained, the ink had run, and the paper had torn at the edges. They looked as forgotten and forlorn as any underfed, under-loved stray. It was a fine photo of Smokey, though. He was - he had been - a very beautiful cat. A plan took shape in Derek's mind, and the next time he was in Jenny's sitting room, he borrowed a photograph of Smokey - a striking image of him in full-body profile - from its place on the cat bookshelves, without telling Jenny and without her noticing.

August arrived, and with it, the birth of the grandchildren twins - a boy and a girl. Their newborn needs and those of her daughter took Jenny's mind from the grief of losing Smokey and her time away from Derek. Derek was away, too, on his cottage holiday in Wales with his sons, his daughters-in-law, and his grandchildren. It was not until September that Jenny's attention turned back to him. He did not mind now, nor was he was worried since he knew how absorbing newborn grandchildren could be.

By mid-September, his surprise gift was ready. He messaged and asked if he could pop around to see her. He had something to give her. It wouldn't take long. She was sorry she'd been so busy. He must stay for a gin and tonic, or a meal if he had time. Yes, he'd like to. The messages pinged from phone to phone in their green and white speech bubbles.

Derek drove to her cottage, along the side of the boulevard, past the flowerbed borders with the drying lavender and the overblown autumnal roses, past the fountain and over the white bridge. In the boot of his car was his gift, too large to carry to her by foot, encased in bubble wrap and carnation-patterned paper.

She was surprised when he gave it to her. She wasn't expecting a present of any sort. They had stopped giving gifts when they saw each other. Wondering, with childlike delight, what he could have brought her, Jenny put the pretty parcel down on the coffee table in the middle of the sitting room to open it. Admiring the paper, she sliced the sellotape carefully with her fingernails so that she could reuse it on a future present. The bubble wrap came away easily and revealed a painting in a frame - a painting of Smokey, modelled from the photograph that had disappeared from its place on the cat shelf.

"Derek," she gasped. "It's beautiful!"

The painting captured Smokey's sleek elegance, alertness, and sophisticated arrogance. There was something almost belle-époque in the design that echoed Smokey's don't care attitude.

"You didn't paint it yourself, did you?"

She had no idea he was a painter.

"No, I didn't. I found a local artist on the internet who specialises in pet portraits, and I hope you don't mind, I borrowed the photo for him to copy to surprise you."

"No, I don't mind. Not at all."

"Do you like it?" he questioned eagerly, stooping forward, grey eyes shining with hope and the desire to please her.

"Yes, I do, Derek. Thank you, I love it."

Putting the painting down, she reached out her arms to him and pulled him into an embrace. Her lips sought his, and she kissed him. He closed his eyes and returned her kisses, breathing in her flowery fragrance. His lilac lady. His garden rose love.

****

And what had happened to poor Smokey?

For weeks, Jenny imagined tearfully that Smokey had met his end, or thought hopefully that a stranger had taken him in, unaware that he had a loving owner far away. Then finally, a few weeks after Derek had given her the striking portrait of her silky smooth cat, she received an email. It was from a young Mum who lived in a village on the other side of the town. A lovely black cat had arrived in her garden over the summer. Her children played with him, they'd bought food and a bed for him and now the whole family loved him as their own. Recently, she'd been given a tattered poster of a missing cat and felt she just had to email to find out if the two cats were one and the same. She attached a photo of Smokey curled up on the lap of a small boy with a huge grin, a toddler girl sitting alongside, stroking Smokey's ebony back.

Jenny's heart melted. "A fitting end to the story," she thought, as she typed her reply and went downstairs to join Derek in her sitting room for their evening gin and tonic.

ACKNOWLEDGEMENTS

Thank you to Peter Waine for inspiring this book with his lovely portraits of imaginary pets and to Stephen Hill for designing the paintings into a cover.

Thank you to Montse Day for helping me with the Spanish phrases and Spanish culture in 'Paco', Alex Price for conversations about 'Guy', Shelagh Fairbank for all her support and especially for comments on 'Smokey', and grateful thanks to Paul Harrison to whom I entrusted the first full version of this book.

Thank you to Kevan Hodges and his team at Ferne Sanctuary, Somerset. This wonderful sanctuary founded by Nina, Lady Hamilton (in my Winnie story) still provides for animals in need today. I am delighted to be an ambassador and to tell people about their work. For more information see www.ferneanimalsanctuary.org.

There are so many pets behind these stories, but I especially want to thank: Sarah Stevens and Shred, Lucy Gravatt and Coni, Lisa Grenfell and Alfie Boe, Sally Trendell and Beau, Hector and Herbie, and our family cats - Fluffy, Phoebe, Polo, Henry, Merlin, and Mystique.

I am blessed to work with a wonderful team at the Endless Bookcase and am grateful to my publisher Carl French, Morgana Evans book and e-book production manager, and Caroline Blackhurst audiobook manager.

Thank you, as always, to my family: Peter, Edgar, Rufus, Conrad, Eloise, Eleanor and Stuart, my wonderful Dad (and cat-lover!), to whom this book is dedicated.

ALSO BY ZOË JASKO

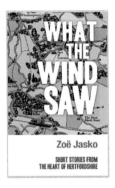

What the Wind Saw is a collection of 25 short stories of the people, real and imagined, from a small tract of ancient land in the heart of Hertfordshire.

The wind has always blown over these villages, fields, rivers, its towns, and its city. It always will. We have the same worries, fear, hopes and dreams today as we have always had.

We are connected to each other by our shared experiences, by the places that we live and by the paths that we tread.

These are stories of friendship, power, love, grief, and ambition inspired by the landscape and what is in it - John Bunyan's Cottage, Shaw's Corner, the annual Ayot St Lawrence aft show, the Devil's Dyke, St Albans market, a walk in the woods, a walk across the fields.

With a Foreword by Robert Voss CBE CStJ, Lord Lieutenant of Hertfordshire.

(The Endless Bookcase, 2022)

The Endless Bookcase: https://theendlessbookcase.com/books/what-the-wind-saw/
Amazon: https://www.amazon.co.uk/dp/B09X1KX36K

1945 Jean Barnet put her war in a box - all her memories, achievements, and heartache. She hoped it would stay there so that she might forget and become the dutiful wife, mother, and daughter a post-war world demanded. Eighteen years later, in 1963, she still hasn't moved on. She knows she must. But in the box is Albert, the gunner she loved and Alice Bragg, the charming socialite who led the Women's Voluntary Service in Cambridge. Will allowing herself to be open to her memories and reinvigorated by the excitement of the wartime years bring Jean the happiness she craves?

Hope is Daffodil Bright weaves the historical biography of Lady Alice Bragg, leader of the W.V.S. and Mayor of Cambridge, with the imagined story of Jean Barnet and her family and friends. It tells how the W.V.S. was founded and the multitude of tasks the volunteers took on. It asks timeless questions about remembering, forgiveness, volunteering for the sake of others, censorship, and self-censorship. With a vivacious cast of actual and fictitious characters, it asserts it is never too late to take from the past the happy and the sad and move on to a brighter tomorrow.

The Endless Bookcase: https://theendlessbookcase.com/books/hope-is-daffodil-bright/
Amazon: https://www.amazon.co.uk/dp/B0BSNMSZVH